Marie Antoinette

Edgar Allan Poe

Charles Baudelaire

Richard Nixon

Franklin D. Roosevelt

Charles Darwin

Graphology Handbook

Curtis W. Casewit

William Shakespeare

John Kennedy

George Washington

Albert Schweitzer

Harry Truman

Napoleon Bonaparte

Benjamin Franklin

Thomas Jefferson

Charles de Gaulle

Whitford Press

1469 Morstein Road
West Chester, Pennsylvania 19380 USA

Graphology Handbook
by Curtis Casewit

International Standard Book Number: 0-914918-15-X
Printed by W.P. on 55-pound Natural shade offset paper.

Published by Whitford Press
Distributed by Schiffer Publishing, Ltd.

This book may be purchased from the publisher.
Please include $2.00 postage.
Try your bookstore first.
Please send for free catalog to:
Whitford Press
c/o Schiffer Publishing, Ltd.
1469 Morstein Road
West Chester, Pennsylvania 19380

Manufactured in the United States of America

Third Printing, July 1987, 3,000 copies
Total copies in print, 11,000

Contents

Introduction

Not long ago, a lady of my acquaintance placed an ad in a singles magazine. "Woman physician, 42," it read, "seeks interesting, sincere, well-educated, sophisticated male companion for dates, travel, possible marriage." She used this method of meeting someone because of her busy medical practice.

I was not surprised when the ad brought eighty replies to her post office box. Nor did it surprise me that she turned to me, an experienced, European-trained graphologist. She had already had one disastrous marriage and this time she wanted to pick the right partner.

She brought me the eighty handwritten letters, asking that I separate the wheat from the chaff and pick out the most suitable men. She told me more about the type of companion she was seeking: no dullards or wolves, no penurious individuals.

Graphology, the study of handwriting, made my task an easy one. I quickly reduced the eighty letters to about thirty, rejecting those which were insincere, selfish, or cold. Then at her request and after more discussion, I further reduced the applicants to the ten best.

During the next few months she dated the ten men I had selected. As she began to know them better, one, an engineer, emerged as the best bet. He was reliable, secure, stable, cultured, and sexually healthy. The profile I had written of the man was apparently so accurate that, even before they met, she felt she knew him. The lady doctor and the engineer will be married soon.

Unusual? Not at all. Consider the following: Daniel Anthony, a leading New York graphologist, startled the audience of *New York*

Magazine with his analysis of an American president whose handwriting hardly changed from the age of 16 to his present age. "He doesn't dare to deviate from the Palmer Method he learned at school," Anthony said about this naive, conservative man. "He lacks flair or imagination." The graphologist showed the same startling perception in his analysis of a high official ("diplomatic duplicity...snakelike manner") and a union boss ("rigidity to the point of stubbornness....").

Felix Lehmann, another colleague of mine, spent months hunting up three different signatures of Richard Nixon (see Chapter 8). One of these, obtained from an autograph dealer, dates back to the late sixties when Nixon was still striving for recognition. "Overpoweringly ambitious...," Lehmann wrote, after analyzing the capitals. The second sample is from the days of Watergate. Lehmann compared the signature with that of Napoleon on St. Helena. "Disintegration. Distrustful." The last signature? "There's nothing left. Only a shadow. His ambitions are over. A shapeless stroke, ambiguity. Total disintegration of personality, a person sinking within himself."

According to a former Central Intelligence Agency official, the CIA employs graphologists whose analysis of the handwritings of Sirhan Sirhan and Lee Harvey Oswald among others, led to their conviction. The former agent stated: "If we saw your writing there was no way to be wrong about you." The Agency's sophisticated methods can work wonders with a simple handwriting sample. Certain diseases can be detected even before their medical diagnosis. Every New Year's Day all the CIA agents in the Soviet Union forward their New Year's cards from Russian friends to CIA headquarters so that the handwriting can be analyzed and filed away.

In many countries of Europe important firms consult graphologists before engaging new personnel. This screening procedure has proven to be very effective. I worked in England as a graphologist for two years, advising large corporations on the merits of individual job applicants. In the United States some large firms require that prospective employees write a few paragraphs by hand; the sample is then submitted to a graphologist.

American graphologists also have made great contributions to the work of the juvenile courts, to teachers who must evaluate slow-learning children, and by working with psychiatrists.

Certainly the case for graphology is an especially strong one on the continent. In Germany, for instance, there are almost as many graphologists as there are dental surgeons. In England, Switzerland, Germany, Austria, and many other countries almost every average adult understands something about graphology and knows that the handwriting of a person expresses the level of intelligence, intellectual qualities, character, talents, and ability (but not, as some people in this country wrongly believe, the future).

What's In it for You?

You will definitely benefit from learning about handwriting analysis. A Chicago school that trains analysts puts it this way: "You can quickly sift from any specimen of handwriting the signs of special talents and aptitudes as well as general character traits. Musical ability...scientific endowments...mathematical proficiency...a bent for management and leadership...skill in handling people...research and investigative capabilities...sound judgment...selling talents—all of these, and more, are brought sharply into focus.

"Hidden fears and frustrations that make people's lives needlessly miserable can be brought to light and examined with sympathetic understanding so that their destructive influence is eliminated." In short, you gain an almost immediate insight into your spouse, lover, parents, boss, or associates.

Analysis becomes an asset in personal relationships. It aids in understanding difficult family members, and in guiding teenagers. Graphology works especially well in vocational counselling; a correct assessment of someone's abilities, whether a son or daughter or friend, can save you thousands of dollars in misspent educational funds.

Moreover, graphology is the best possible tool with which to know your own character traits, motivations, and drives. Nietzsche, the German philosopher, claimed that few individuals actually know themselves:

> ...Ich Kenne mancher Menschen Sinn,
> Und weiss nicht, wer ich selber bin!
> Mein Auge ist mir viel zu nah,
> Ich bin nicht, was ich seh' und sah!...
>
> ...Many human minds I know,
> While my SELF I do ignore,

My own eye is much too near,
What I am is not quite...

Graphology proves especially valuable to you in business. Analysis cuts through appearances and lets you see a person as he or she really is. The first impression a person makes is sometimes deceptive, and even the experienced psychologist is often mistaken when judging someone at first sight. To cite a few examples: Weak-minded, feeble, and cowardly persons often mask their personality by assuming energetic and aggressive slang. A high intellectual forehead is sometimes not in proportion with genuine mental qualities. Even a skilled observer may be falsely impressed by what a French writer called *un front large et haut comme une portique* (a forehead as large and high as an archway).

Thieves and liars often are capable of looking you straight in the eye, giving a false impression of honesty, but their handwriting tells the truth. That is perhaps why some credit managers rely on handwriting analysis. Personality characteristics such as honesty or deceit, pride or sloth, will-power or the lack of it, conservatism or wastefulness, all play a part in the determination of a good credit risk or a bad one. An inspection of the applicant's handwriting saves the credit supervisor both time and money.

Checking a job applicant's suitability before he or she is hired saves thousands of dollars in training the wrong person. Some sales managers have long used the services of graphologists. "I found them a tremendous asset in selecting salesmen," writes the branch manager of Business Men's Assurance Company. "Without the benefit of interpretation of their handwriting, I probably would not have hired some of these people; because, on the surface they appeared to be average prospective salesmen such as the many I will interview in any given month... and yet, their handwriting revealed them to be exceptional people. After hiring these particular individuals, I have been very pleased with the results, and most of them have proven themselves to be exactly what the graphologist said they would."

Graphology: A Science

Graphology has nothing to do with ESP, the occult, or fortune telling. You cannot predict the future by looking at someone's handwriting. Nor does graphology encourage amateur psychologizing. Moreover, only charlatans, not genuine graphologists, operate at fairs, carnivals, or Coney Island.

(Gypsies who offer to analyze your handwriting should be equally distrusted.) Instead, graphology falls within the domain of the European-trained psychologist and the U.S. clinical psychologist. According to James C. Crumbaugh of the Veterans Administration Hospital in Gulfport, Mississippi, "Several studies indicate that handwriting analysis is as well validated as 'many other projective techniques of personality assessment currently in use' and in fact has '*definite advantages* over most other clinical tests.' It's especially adaptable to studies of reluctant patients, and no extra time is required for administering the test."

Dr. A.A. Roback of Harvard University, a scholar who has authored 40 books, has said: "Thus far I have not encountered a single individual who, after considerable application of graphology, has rejected it as unscientific."

The above may explain why police officers, judges, and lawyers put so much credence in handwriting experts. In law, the science has proven its worth time and time again. An attorney may assess character traits of clients; a prosecutor can gain an accurate picture of the person being prosecuted. Handwriting is invaluable in resolving signatures in questioned documents. It is used to determine forgeries on checks. Handwriting analysis lends authenticity to identification of extortion notes.

How Does Graphology Work?

Neurologists and graphologists have long agreed that one's handwriting begins in the brain, which transmits signals through the motor cortex and the central nervous system to the hand. The result is a most individual one, much like one's electrocardiogram. It thus makes sense that severely ill people will write differently from healthy people. In the same vein, a hyperactive person will have a different script from a calm individual. Handwriting, in short, points to the inner person. One might call writing a gesture, which can express all the deeply felt emotions, the passions and enthusiasms, or, conversely, restraint and coolness. Certainly it puts one's feelings on physical record, which can then be examined at leisure.

To the trained expert, no handwriting sample resembles another, just as no two fingerprints are the same. Indeed, the tremendous variety of letter formations, strokes, and other connective forms—as well as the individual use of space, margins, and script size—may offer the best proof that graphology has to work. How different we all are! The variety of handwriting, like that of postage stamps, prompted some pre-teen children in Switzerland to collect hundreds of samples. (According to Dr. Max Pulver, such collection instincts later resulted in a serious graphological interest.)

The enormous variety of graphic expressions can best be seen in the contrasting samples given in Figures 1-7.

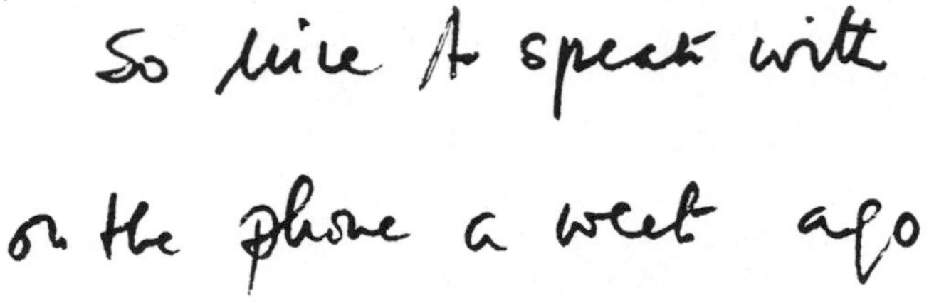

Figure 1.

Figure 2.

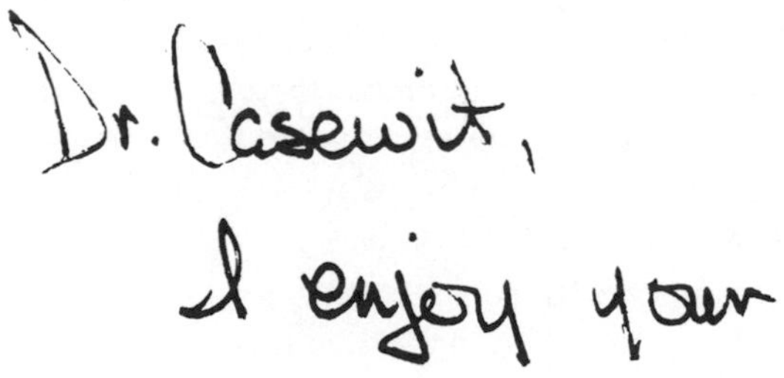

Figure 3.

"Miss Pitt", and

Figure 4.

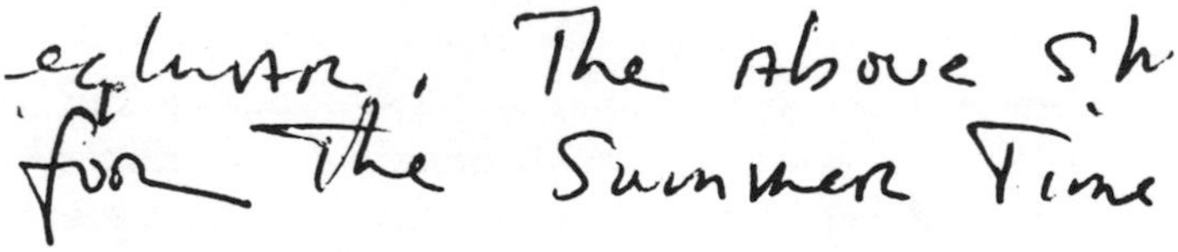

[illegible], The above sh
for the Summer Time

Figure 5.

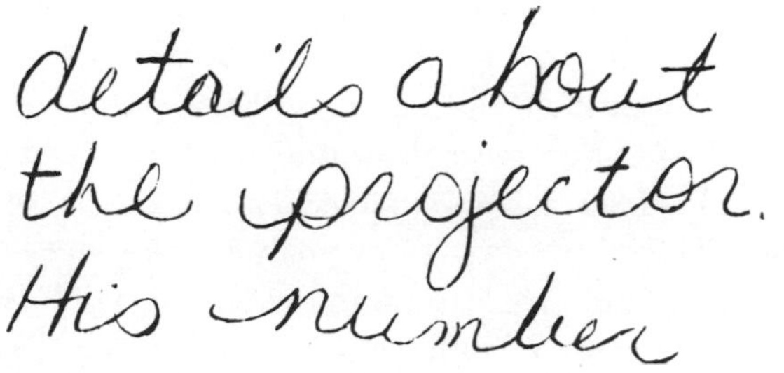

details about
the projector.
His number

Figure 6.

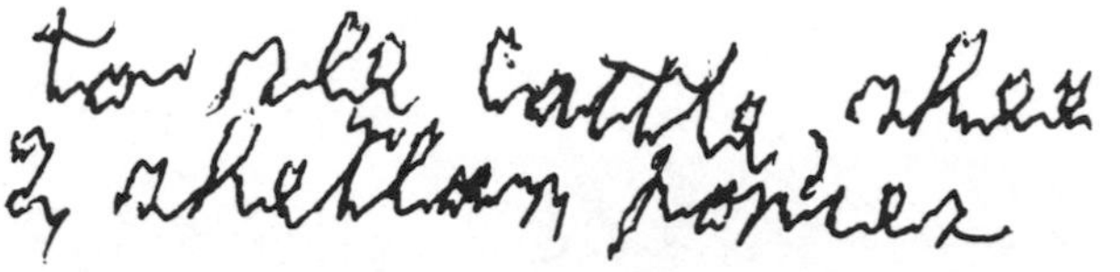

Figure 7.

Some Historical Notes

An introduction to graphology would not be complete without a look into its history. The late M.N. Bunker, one of America's first and foremost authorities in the field, did a superb job in finding some early mentions of penmanship and its deeper meanings. Bunker points to what may be the earliest recorded reference to handwriting analysis: The Greek philosopher Aristotle (384-322 B.C.) wrote that handwriting is a symbol of speech and speech is a symbol of mental experience. We can interpret this as meaning that Aristotle observed that thought and personality are reflected in a person's handwriting. The Roman Emperor Nero (A.D. 37-68) is reported to have remarked when pointing out a man at court: "His writing shows him to be treacherous." And some time later on, during the second century, the Roman historian Suetonius wrote about the handwriting of Emperor Augustus, tying it in to his character.

Organized systems of handwriting analysis did not emerge until the seventeenth century. In 1622 an Italian scholar and physician, Camillo Baldi, while professor at the University of Bologna, published a book titled *Treatise on a Method to Recognize the Nature and Quality of a Writer from His Letters*. It stirred up a considerable amount of interest among the educated classes. However, handwriting analysis could not be used widely because only a few people could read and write. As M.N. Bunker stated: "Typically, analysis continued to interest the intellectuals." The next work published was by Johann Kaspar Lavater (1741-1801), a Swiss scholar and writer on personality, who was connected with the University of Zurich.

During the century after the publication of Lavater's book, handwriting analysis became almost too popular among writers, artists, statesmen, and other public figures. Using more art than science, handwriting analysis was practiced (sometimes with amazing intuitive skill) by Goethe, Poe, the Brownings, Leibnitz, Balzac, Dickens, Madame de Stael, and others. The story goes that Thomas Gainsborough, one of the greatest of all English artists, achieved the lifelike quality of his portraits by having before him, while painting, a handwriting specimen of the subject. He explained that the handwriting enabled him to capture the very essence of the subject's personality.

To be sure, the British upheld Gainsborough's theory. Sir Walter Scott (1771-1832), a contemporary of Gainsborough, aptly described, in *Canongate*, the author of a manuscript he was about to toss into the fire: "That neat but crowded and constrained small hand argued a man of good conscience, well-regulated passions, and, to use his own phrase, an upright walk in life; but it also indicated narrowness of spirit, inveterate prejudice, and hinted at some degree of intolerance. . . and the flourished capital letters which ornamented the commencement of each paragraph, do they not express forcibly the pride and sense of importance with which the author undertook and accomplished his task? I persuaded myself the whole was so complete a portrait of the man, that it would not have been a more undutiful act to have defaced his picture."

The term *graphology* was first used by a French abbé, Jean-Hippolyte Michon, who proceeded on a more scientific basis in 1871. In France some serious study had been done by Abbé Louis J. H. Flandrin, the Bishop of Amiens, and the Archbishop of Cambrai. Their greatest contribution to handwriting analysis, however, was the training of their assistant, Abbé Michon. In 1875, Michon published what was up to that time the most scholarly work on handwriting analysis, *The Practical System of Graphology*, and thus coined the generic name, graphology. Michon was a tireless worker. He examined thousands of handwriting samples in order to make a list of hundreds of individual graphic signs that were supposed to identify individual personality traits, a system that came to be known as "the school of fixed signs."

A French graphologist, Crepieux-Jamin, developed the first workable and practical theory of handwriting analysis, called the "trait-stroke," in 1896. This entailed determination of a person's individuality, including personality, goals, subconscious thought processes, and character traits.

It is to Crepieux-Jamin's credit that, near the turn of the century, he interested Alfred Binet, the eminent psychologist, in the subject of handwriting analysis as a personality testing technique. In 1905, several years before publishing his first intelligence test, Binet experimented with handwriting analysis, using seven analysts. He gave each of them the handwriting of 37 men who had been highly successful in life and 37 men from the same social level who had not been outstanding. Binet then asked the analysts to tell him which samples belonged to the famous men. One of the experts achieved an amazing score of 92 percent accuracy. The others made scores of 86, 83, 80, 68, 66, and 61—all well above the chance level. Even with the rather primitive techniques of that early day, graphology proved surprisingly successful. In other studies, Binet was able to determine the intelligence and honesty of his subjects from their script.

Important scientific advances in graphology were occurring at this time in Germany. Dr. Wilhelm Preyer, a German professor, first discovered that handwriting emanated from the brain and that graphology was a helpmate of psychology. Dr. Preyer published his famous *Zur Psychologie Des Schreibens* (*About The Psychology of Writing*) in 1895. Preyer, a professor of physiology, held the attention of his colleagues, just as another German, Dr. Georg Meyer, a medical man and psychiatrist, impressed the profession when he required his patients to write a sample before he would talk to them. The result was an important book titled *Die Wissenschaftlichen Grundlagen der Graphologie* (*The Scientific Basis for Graphology*).

The man who made the greatest contribution to the advance of graphology as a science was Ludwig Klages, a German philosopher. He was the real pioneer of graphology, the man who most fully explored the subject. His theories, embodied in the masterpiece, *Die Handschrift*, (*The Handwriting*) created new ideas that inspired many of his successors. Klages discovered that the possession of several characteristics will inevitably bestow an additional one. For instance, the "talent of adaption" results from the following qualities: sensitiveness, refinement of feeling, versatility, intellectual flexibility, self-domination, and sociability. Some of his definitions are remarkably original, for example, "Jealousy is the egoism of love."

Moreover, credit must be given to Ludwig Klages for applying the gestalt theory to graphology; that is, for seeing a handwriting sample first as an integrated whole, before examining its components. Klages invented the term expressive movement, meaning all the common activities that the average person performs almost automatically, without conscious thought: walking, running, talking, gestures, facial expression, and most especially handwriting. He also invented the *Formniveau* or FN (the form level), that is, the *overall quality* of one's writing. Thus he was able to increase the scientific prestige of graphology.

Klages' influence on handwriting analysis in Germany soon spread elsewhere. In Zurich, Switzerland, Dr. Max Pulver (1889-1952), who was associated with the prestigious Institute for Applied Psychology, was soon adding to graphology the flavor of analytic psychology. His work, *Symbolik* der Handschrift, (*Symbolism of the Handwriting*), became well-known and it influenced many modern graphologists, including this writer. (I met Dr. Max Pulver in Zurich shortly after World War II and found him helpful and amiable.) Pulver was an associate and friend of Dr. Carl Jung and a colleague of Dr. Hermann Rorschach, after whom the famous ink blot test was named. Dr. Pulver made news with the discovery that criminality, sexual difficulties, and physical problems could all be seen in the strokes of the pen.

In the United States, graphology remained somewhat unknown until after World War I. Much of the credit for its arrival on these shores goes to M.N. Bunker. Bunker published his first article on handwriting in 1911. The publisher, and presumably his readers, liked the material so well that Bunker was commissioned to write a series titled "The Pen is Mightier. . ."

In the early 1930s, Gordon W. Allport and Phillip Vernon, psychology professors at Harvard, conducted a considerable amount of experimental work. They concluded that "graphic movement (handwriting) is not activity dissociated from the complexities of personality, but seems to be intricately woven with deep-lying determinants of conduct. Critics who flatly say 'there is nothing in handwriting analysis' are wrong. Many studies, in fact, show . . . that handwriting analysis does identify personality characteristics."

M.N. Bunker was among the first to depart from the generic term *graphology* in favor of *graphoanalysis*. The formal study of graphoanalysis began in 1929 when Bunker founded a school of handwriting analysis. Like graphology, graphoanalysis still meant the delineation of personality traits through handwriting. It became the registered trademark of the International Graphoanalysis Society, headquartered in Chicago. The IGS boasts of thousands of members. Certainly it represents the American success story: Correspondence courses and diplomas sell at $600 each. The IGS avoided the term *graphology*; it instructed students to interpret strokes and letters and not to look at the entire picture. ("It's how you cross your t's that show character traits," reads one IGS propaganda story.) Some of the IGS trainees feel that they, as graphoanalysts, operate on the same principle as the original graphologists. But most of the European experts, both on the continent and now in the United States, disagree. Felix Lehmann, a dean among German graphology elite, puts it this way: "The Graphoanalysis system is like describing a person's body without giving recognition to the soul which sheds light and gives life to the body."

Apart from the term *graphoanalysis*, other groups and individuals have used names like *graphotherapeutics*, *psychographology*, *scriptology*, and *graphodiagnosis*.

Among the Americans, the most interesting (and reliable) work was and still is being done by Daniel Anthony, who does not object to the old-fashioned term *graphologist*. One of his achievements was to persuade the New School for Social Research, an accredited college in New York City, to offer graphology as part of their curriculum.

Anthony has elevated handwriting analysis to a science, and I must thank him for assisting me with this book, which was also enriched by the counsel and help of other respected graphologists. Among them are two former Europeans, Felix Lehmann and Felix Klein, of New York City.

Curtis Casewit
University of Colorado
Denver Center
February, 1980

1

The Handwriting Sample

A skilled, experienced graphologist can peel back the layers of a personality and look deeply into a human being. Character strengths, talents, reliability, sincerity, kindness, warmth, persistence, and willpower can all be delineated, along with other traits that make up an individual. This book introduces you to the telltale signs of dishonesty, hypocrisy, egotism, narcissism, and, for the benefit of personnel managers, lack of industry, laziness, boredom, ruthlessness, and thievery. Many graphologists have been able to warn women that they see in the handwriting of a possible companion an unsuitable prospect.

This book presents the material with complete honesty and provides a tool for evaluating friends, partners, customers, and employees. The strokes of a pen reveal the chronically insecure, the neurotic, or the mentally ill. (Chapter 6 provides data on the writing of schizophrenics and other sick persons.) Some excellent work has also been done in the fields of physical health. You will learn how to detect possible circulatory problems, heart disease, and the ravages of old age, sexual dysfunctions, or extreme physical weakness.

To judge a handwriting sample you must be in possession of at least a full page or more. In fact, three to four pages (in letter form) work out best. For a detailed, thorough analysis, it would be best to secure some letters that date back several years, as well as samples of recent weeks. The chronological spread gives you a chance to observe the physical and character development of a person.

It is easy to spot charlatans or amateurs because they ask for only one line of writing. A few written words will do in a pinch, if no additional writing is available, but an analysis in depth always requires at least a page of material. Occasionally a quick analysis of an extremely interesting person can be made with the help of only a few paragraphs.

The paper should not be lined. You must be able to see how the writer handles space. Descending scripts have an altogether different meaning from ascending ones. The paper should not have a marked margin: Let the writer decide on how far to go on the right, the left, and the top. The amount of white space helps you interpret character. Keep in mind that the paper should be placed on an appropriate surface: A hard surface like a school chair or wooden table may yield an inadequate sample. A magazine, file folder, or book is helpful in obtaining clearer writing. In the same vein, the writer should not stand but should be comfortably seated.

Should you ask the person to write slowly or rapidly? I always encourage people to put down their thoughts, or copy from a book, quickly. Interestingly, the most valid analysis can be given for the material that is at the bottom of a written page. By that time, the hand is warmed up and the writing has become natural enough for an accurate analysis. A pen, by the way, is better than a pencil. The latter smudges.

Some people say: My handwriting is never the same—once it is straight, once slanting, once going up, once going down, and so on. To the graphologist these changes make no difference. Compare handwriting to a face: Although the expression is not always the same, although one sometimes smiles or sometimes frowns, the underlying features remain unchanged. The same applies to handwriting. By the same token, the more material you have the better.

There are some other important points.

Some Warnings

When a handwriting sample is to be analyzed, there still is a need to ask for the person's age. After all, you are entitled to know if a man or woman is seventy years old and writes like a young person of 30 or if a 30-year-old has the handwriting of someone seventy. The same naturally applies to young people.

The writer should also state his or her sex. Many readers might object to this idea. These skeptics will say that a graphologist ought to be able to determine one's sex. This is not true and the explanation is clear: There are masculine types of females and feminine types of males. How can the graphologist be expected to know which is which? In fact, a prior knowledge of the gender will assist the analyst in telling much about someone's sexuality.

When one contacts a professional graphologist, one should not be astonished if he or she wants to know some of the reasons for the analysis. Is a prospective mate's character being checked? Is one's own talent for a profession being examined? Does one want to know if a business contact is a good risk for a loan? Explanations will help guide the professional graphologist.

Newcomers to the field often make the mistake of reading the sample. This is wrong, of course, because a graphologist must not be influenced by words or messages. Only the actual writing itself counts.

Prior knowledge of someone's profession is also helpful. To be sure, a bricklayer who seldom writes cannot be judged by the same yardstick as a professor who handles the pen every day. The worker's penmanship may be less skilled, and he or she may be relatively uneducated. This should be taken into account. Experts also warn that ethnic origins make a difference and should be mentioned in advance. For instance, if one grew up in Germany prior to World War II, one would write in a somewhat angular, Gothic script. To some degree the angularity may remain and should be taken into consideration. If such sharp angles occur in an American script, a graphologist would interpret it altogether differently. The graphologist should also know if a person is a lefthander.

It is difficult to disguise a handwriting; the professional graphologist spots the fake at once and then proceeds to make the analysis from the natural formations.

Is the Handwriting Unique?

It is an intriguing rule of graphology that interesting personalities, leaders, and truly mature persons always discard some of the penmanship they learned early in life. Their script becomes more individualistic, more unusual. They write according to the dictates of their nature. The truly creative jettison many of the forms first taught them as children. Instead, these artists, thinkers, and scientists create their own capitals and letters.

Figures 8, 9, and 10 are excellent examples of Americans who departed from the script they learned in school.

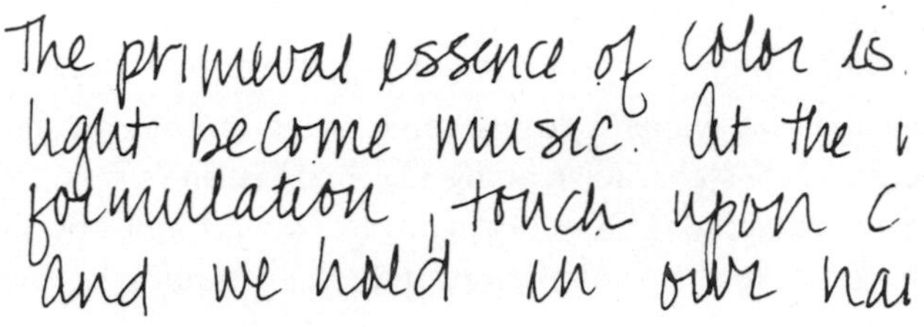

The primeval essence of color is
light become music. At the
formulation, touch upon
and we hold in our ha

Figure 8.

---

whom I admire greatly

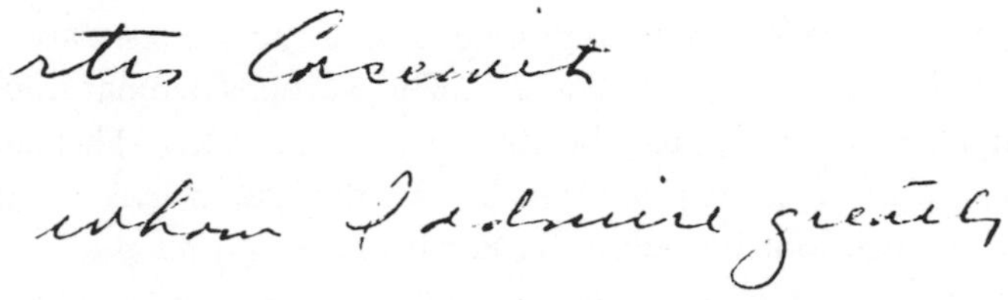

Figure 9.

Go placidly amid the
and remember what

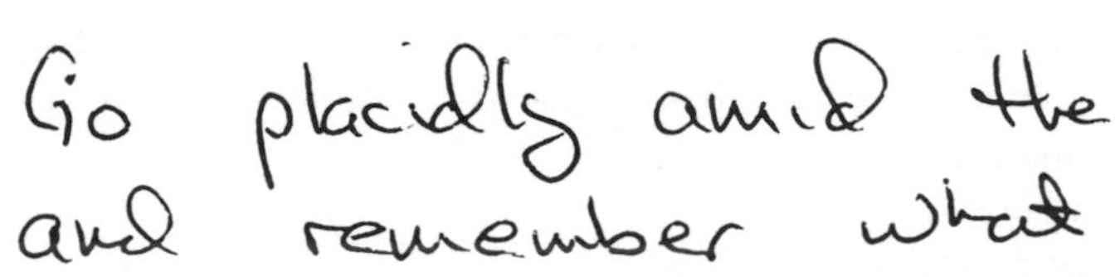

Figure 10.

In contrast, some writers stick to the stereotyped letters they were taught in the early grades. There is nothing wrong in holding on to the norms, but such people are usually more conventional, more banal, and bound by the rules of society. They are nice people, but unwilling to blaze their own trail or try new approaches. They are less adventurous. Figures 11 and 12 disclose such persons.

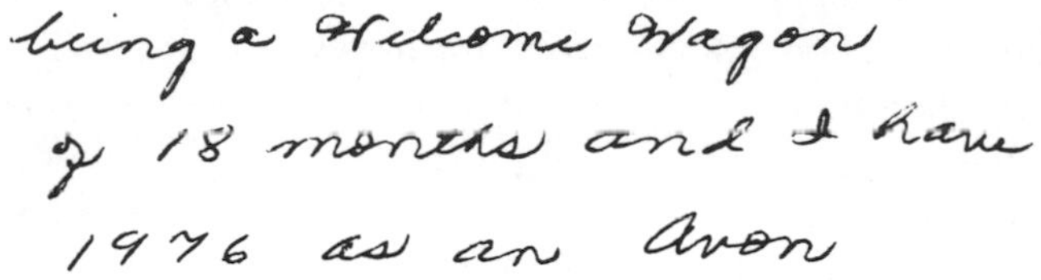

Figure 11.

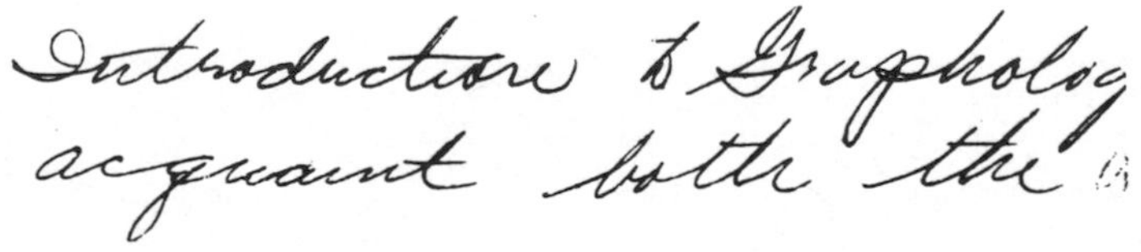

Figure 12.

Your own background is important in learning graphology. I am convinced that anyone who is interested in other human beings can acquire the basics outlined in this book. It takes no special talent, just interest. The rules are simple enough to learn, as the following chapters will show. There is a difference between the budding graphologist, who reveals a few secrets of his friends at a cocktail party, and a serious, foolproof analysis. The latter is possible only if you invest some extra time in the study of graphology by: 1) collecting many samples of handwriting; 2) keeping in practice by actually analyzing scripts every day; and 3) reading books on psychology. A good background in psychology is essential for advanced graphology. It does not mean that you must attend university studies; simply read books on human behavior and character structure. Some of the tables and charts in this book will prove helpful.

A Sample Analysis

A graphologist can visualize a complete human being from a general impression of a handwriting, followed by a closer look at the slant, margins, motion of lines, width, size, pressure, connections between letters, sizes and shapes of capitals, beginnings and ends of words, space between words, and individual letter formations. All of the above will yield a composite picture of a personality. Good graphologists are honest and candid, letting the chips of information fall where they may, even if the analyzed person has many negative traits. This book will proceed with total candor.

What is an analysis like? The characterization of Rita R. is based on the handwriting sample given in Figure 13.

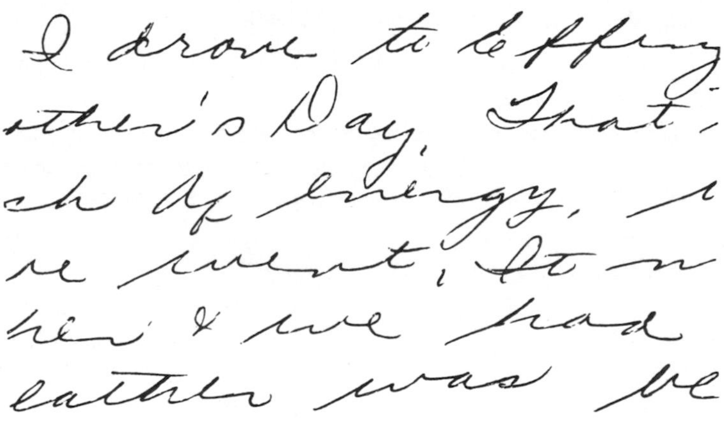

Figure 13.

Rita R. Female. American. Age: 41

Some of the outstanding qualities of this woman are her capacity for warmth, her affection, her ability to feel and to experience in depth. She is much more of a romantic than most American women of our age, and at times, her handwriting gives the impression that she is obsessed with love. (A poet once wrote that man's love is but a toy, compared to woman's, whose love "is her whole existence.") Her sexuality is healthy, and, while strongly sexed, she also reaches out in other areas, generously giving of her time, always willing to assist others (even if she is never repaid), trying hard to make friends.

Such friendships will be rewarded, of course, since Rita R. is basically kind, sincere, honest, reliable, good-willed, and somewhat strong. Her naturalness, her freshness, her gregariousness and vivaciousness—her truly social nature—must be a great asset in her private and professional life. Such qualities, especially in combination with physical attractiveness, act as a magnet, so that she will never lack people around her.

On the positive side, too, one must take note of Rita R.'s sense of adventure, her need for excitement, her capacity for Joy (which is capitalized on purpose) and, in a man-woman relationship, her sudden bursts of unrepressed passion. A great deal of energy (in all spheres), a fine resiliency, which allows her to bounce back from misadventures, and a healthy though not extreme selfishness that allows her to help others are all good qualities.

Indeed, there can be no doubt that Rita R. is her own person, and, while capable of love, still requires a modicum of independence and her own private spaces. Moreover, she needs to be in the center of things, and to function well requires approval from others. She cannot be hemmed in, physically or personally, and whatever her devotion to a relationship, she will demand to, and is entitled to, pursue her own profession. (There is no indication of sexual promiscuousness in the handwriting.)

Her intelligence and taste are definitely above average. And because she has both feet on the ground she will always be able to earn her living.

How about the negative aspects of Rita's personality?

An overall impression of the handwriting, that is, the first gestalt of it, shows a sawing movement across the paper. Her pen pressure and speed are tremendous, with lower loops sometimes "sawing" into the next lines. This indicates a *potential* ruthlessness. If things go well between her and a man, fine, but woe to him if things go badly! The possible ruthlessness can also lead to occasional pushiness, an attempt to dominate another person, as shown by certain pen strokes.

This is the writing of someone who will embark on an adventure without thinking it through completely, or will spend money impulsively. It indicates an occasionally impulsive nature.

Should a particular man marry this woman? That depends on the man, of course. He must be able to cope with a woman who will occasionally blow off steam. (Her angers dissipate, however, and she never stockpiles her grievances.) In extreme cases, under severe provocation, the man must expect great fury, even to the extent of minor violence. (Dishes may be thrown.) While that may rarely occur, especially if the man is placating and peace-making, Rita may be too high-strung on some occasions, and too excitable on others. These traits and possibilities, along with her magnificent bursts of passion may emerge only after a long and close relationship.

The Overall Picture

One of the major differences between graphoanalysis and European graphology is the graphologist's search for the overall picture, the general impression of a script. Psychiatrists may call it a search for the gestalt, the total image. One begins with the whole and not with the details, such as how a person crosses the t-bars or dots the i's. One at first ignores how the writer loops the f's or g's. The size of a script or even its legibility remain unimportant at this juncture.

Only the overall picture counts. Klages, the great German graphologist who has contributed so much to what we know today, called it the "attitude" of a handwriting. He compared it once to his first glançe at a famous painting, and how it affected him. From this general feeling about a script, Klages moved to a less subjective judgment.

He began to search for the quality in a handwriting. Klages called it the "Formniveau," which means the achievement level of a script, or simply its quality. Ever since Klages' discovery, all graphologists stress the Formniveau approach. Your entire analysis of a person's hand will hinge on it.

Here are some specifics.

A superior handwriting, in Klages' opinion, meant a harmonious handwriting. It has a sense of order. There is symmetry in how the lines and words are arranged on the page. A high Formniveau means clarity and perhaps beauty. There are no graphic extremes such as lines that bang and cut into one another, capitals that streak in all directions, or stormy shifts of slant. Instead, all is well balanced on the page. Regularity rules.

A high-caliber Formniveau will also pursue a steady rhythm. (The word means "flow" in Greek.) A good rhythm tolerates no interruptions, no slowing down, no abrupt pauses or sudden accelerations. Rhythm, in short, implies repetition and a certain amount of speed. Extremes in any part of a handwriting diminish the rhythm, of course, and bring about a less positive picture. Nor can there be a steady musical beat in a disjointed, fractured, chaotic handwriting. The latter would have to be classified less positively, too: Its Formniveau could not be superior.

The assessment of a person's Formniveau happens to be one of the few items in graphology that cannot be learned in one easy lesson. It takes some experience. You gain it by comparing various scripts. Look for balance. Is there a sense of order? Does the handwriting derail somewhere, or does it travel serenely? Is there enough harmony? Can you detect a rhythmic motion of the writer's hand, or does it appear to be halting, with varied pressure of the pen on paper, with ink splotches and so on?

A few good examples show some fine writing. Indeed, there is excellent rhythm and superior Formniveau in Figures 14, 15, and 16. Despite the differing ages and personalities of the writers, the quality is uniformly superb. The pen moves steadily across the paper. The spaces between lines or words hardly vary.

Rhythm is an important portion of the quality, and I shall mention some of the results of exhaustive studies on rhythm done by Felix Klein, a New York graphologist.

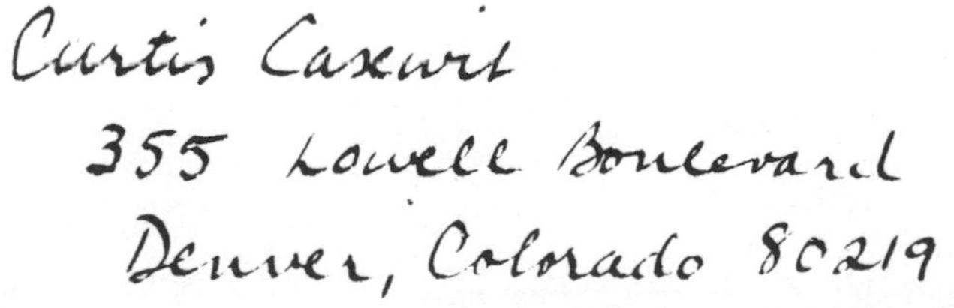

Curtis Caxwit
355 Lowell Boulevard
Denver, Colorado 80219

Figure 14.

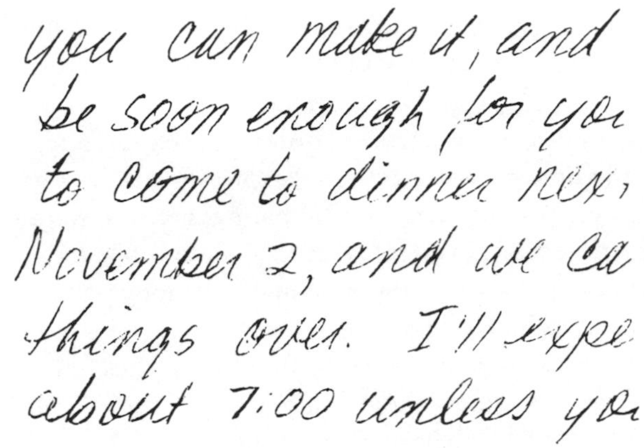

you can make it, and
be soon enough for you
to come to dinner nex,
November 2, and we ca
things over. I'll expe
about 7:00 unless you

Figure 15.

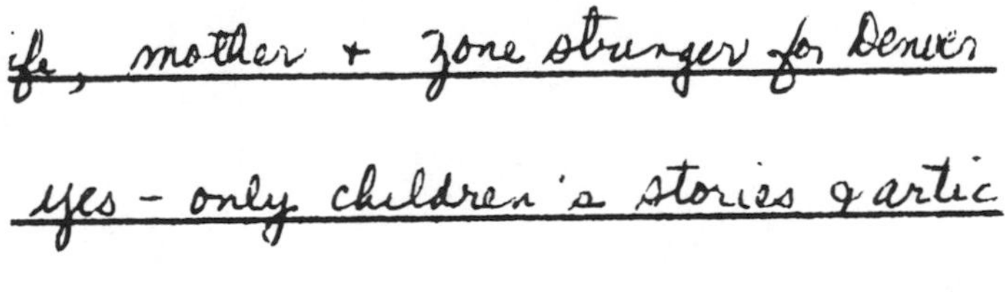

ife, mother + Zone stranger for Denver
yes - only children's stories & artic

Figure 16.

Klein adds valid information concerning rhythm. In a lecture delivered to many of his colleagues, Klein suggested the following: "Rhythm is disturbed by an uneven distribution of words and lines on the page." He also pointed out other areas:

> Internal harmony of margins. We do not expect an equal margin on the left and on the right side; in fact this would be highly unusual. But the margins should show some kind of proportion.

Harmony of spaces between lines. Very large spaces between lines, or very small ones, do not increase the rhythmic picture. It goes without saying that the size of the writing must be taken into consideration when judging the space between lines.

Searching for extremes in the handwriting. The following extremes in handwriting are disturbing to the rhythm:

Irregular pressure

Predominance of one zone over another

Extreme irregularity, which does not permit any pattern at all

Extreme differences in size

Extreme differences in slant

Any extreme in the handwriting speaks against rhythm.

The specimens in Figures 17, 18, and 19 from my own collection show some inferior Formniveau writings.

In all three cases, the first overall impression is a negative one: the graphic picture always appears erratic and badly organized. In every instance, the rhythm is disturbed. The spacing is poor. Graphic excesses such as the oversized capitals and balloon-like letter formations in Figure 17, or the whipping motions and collapses of Figure 18, all contribute to the lower evaluation.

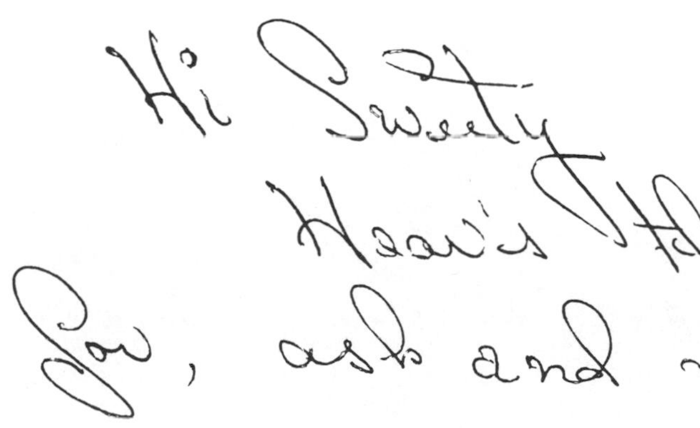

Figure 17.

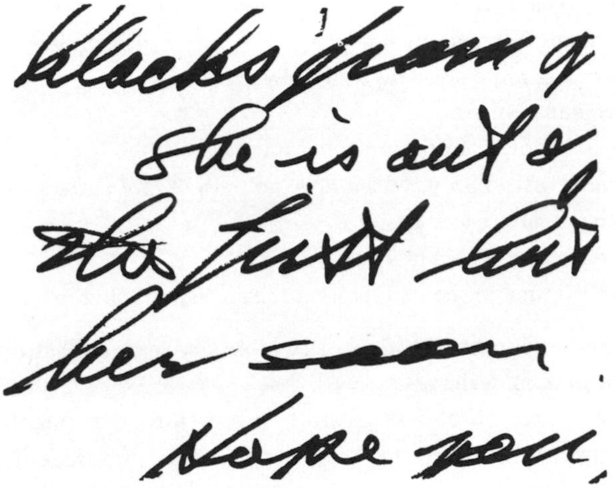

Figure 18.

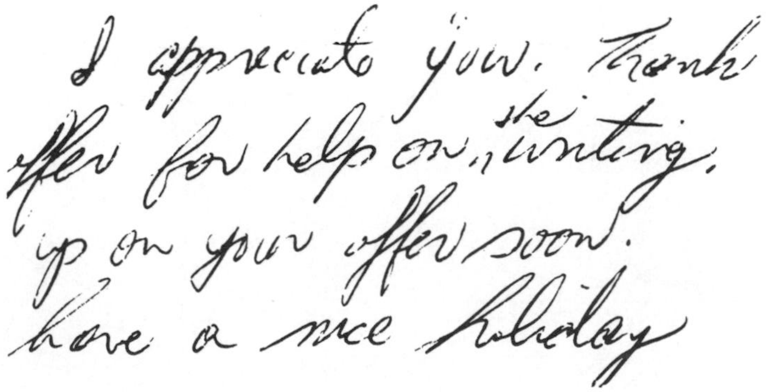

Figure 19.

Originality

The grade of an individual's Formniveau is influenced by one more item, originality. Originality could well mean simplification; that is, an absence of adornment. Some of the world's greatest minds—Einstein, Churchill, Bergson—often produced the simplest penmanship.

The trend toward simplification should put a script into a higher level. The writer has created his or her own style of writing, irrespective of what was learned at school. This denotes creativity, and the attempt to take the shortest route (as in Figures 20 and 21) always points to a direct, practical mind. The stripping of all ornamentation shows up especially well in capitals such as the I (which represents the ego), T, F, M, and many others. The use of block letters and printing often adds to a pleasant first impression of a handwriting. True originality aims for uniqueness, of course; in a high Formniveau, however, the overall balance and beauty will remain undisturbed.

It can be difficult for a beginning graphologist to rate a writer's quality level. You must practice the FN assessment. Learn to evaluate the Formniveau because your entire analysis begins with it. For the sake of clarity, graphology instructors use a Formniveau grade. The highest, awarded only to the best specimen, will be an FN 5. The lowest (or poorest FN showing) will be an FN 1. An FN 4 is excellent, of course, and even an FN 3 is desirable. An FN 2½ would be average, and an FN 2 is below par.

Please note that graphologists, like psychiatrists or psychologists, avoid value judgments. They never use the words "good" or "bad" in their interpretations of someone's character based on Formniveau. Instead, they prefer to say a handwriting is of superior (or lesser) quality. A first-rate FN is associated with more positive (+) traits; an inferior FN results in more negative characteristics. (Indicated by a minus sign [−].)

It is intriguing to note that the scientific aspects of graphology become evident when you ask three different professionals to grade the FN of a person. The three practitioners will probably come up with the same results. After all, they all judge an FN by the same standards. The graphologists all look for harmony, balance, simplicity and rhythm. It benefits the beginner to test his mettle with some typical scripts, award FN grades, and then check the answers.

Here are FN evaluations of some handwriting samples. The figure number appears first, with the grade in parentheses: Figure 1 (4), Figure 8

(*5*), Figure 9 (*5*), Figure 10 (*4*), Figure 14 (*5*), Figure 13 (*3*), Figure 19 (*2*) and Figure 18 (*1*).

The Formniveau: Applications

Why should you learn how to rate the FNs yourself?—because so much depends on whether a script is superior or inferior. Indeed, almost all graphological interpretations hinge upon the FN principle. Analyze some examples. In a low-grade (FN 2 or FN 1) writing, delicate pen pressure, especially when it occurs in concert with broken letters, signifies weakness. In a superior writing, however (FN 5 or FN 4) lack of pressure means sensitivity and consideration for others, particularly when certain other signs are present.

The importance of first judging quality must be stressed repeatedly. Here are some examples:

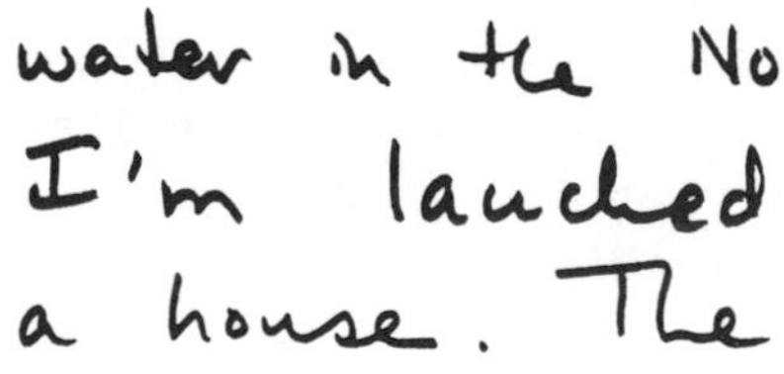

Figure 20.

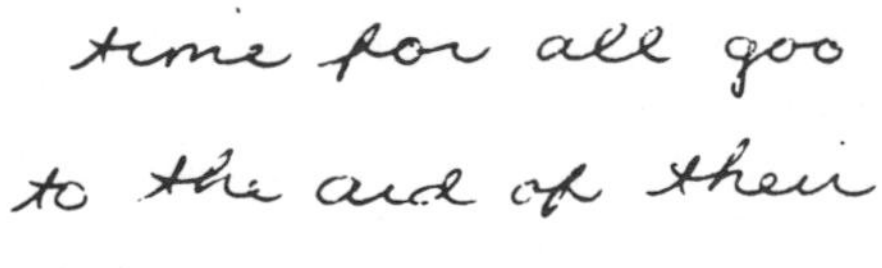

Figure 21.

In the case of a lesser Formniveau, sharp angles usually denote that the person is critical in a negative sense: malicious, nasty, or unpleasant. Angularity can also mean pugnaciousness. Boxing movements will be seen in the handwriting.

The opposite of sharpness is roundness, of course. Take an extremely round script in a well balanced, harmonious, pleasant handwriting with a high FN grade. The roundness would indicate someone who is adaptable, kindly, warm, and easygoing.

In a low-caliber hand, however, extreme roundness suggests a naive person, a pushover.

One could find many other illustrations for the dual possibilities. Complex? Not so. Psychologists point out that any trait can be exaggerated to such an extent that it is no longer desirable. Modesty may thus turn into an inferiority complex; pride can become conceit.

Paul de Ste. Colombe, one of the leading French graphologists, developed an excellent table illustrated below, to show how interpretations of the high FN vary from those of the low FN.

Some handwritings have neither a superior nor an inferior FN but fall somewhere in between. In these cases the expert seeks additional clues in the script. These clues will be discussed in the following chapters.

HANDWRITING TYPE	SUPERIOR FN	INFERIOR FN
Small	Good concentration	Pettiness
Light	Delicacy, spirituality	Debility
Fast	Spontaneity, vivacity	Impetuosity
Sinuous	Diplomacy	Prevarication, ruse
Disconnected	Intuition	Illogic

2

Slant, Size and Zones

After a cursory glance and a Formniveau evaluation, you will find it easy enough to check whether a script is even or uneven. Dr. Max Pulver always felt that an analysis can proceed logically from the general impression to the more specific fluctuations in the upper and lower spheres of a handwriting sample. Are there many changes of direction? Does the writer vary the height of small letters, that is, the middle zones? Do the margins shift? Or is the opposite the case? Do the lines waver or do they go up or down? In fact, does the handwriting appear too even? Is it too mechanical and slow? Extreme, nonflowing regularity often results in a rigid, boring picture which is not harmonious but is artificial. So is the person, of course.

Figure 22 presents a typical case.

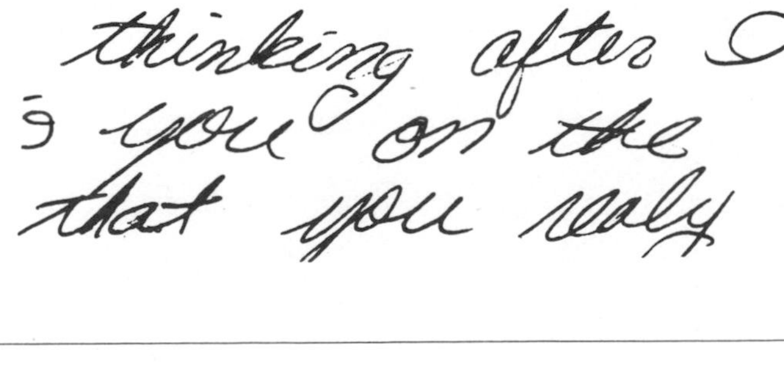

Figure 22.

You can easily see that the words were written with such painstaking care that they have become lifeless. At the other extreme, Figure 23 reaches the zenith of unevenness. The writer is obviously an emotional person whose moods can vary between exaltation and depression (note constant changes).

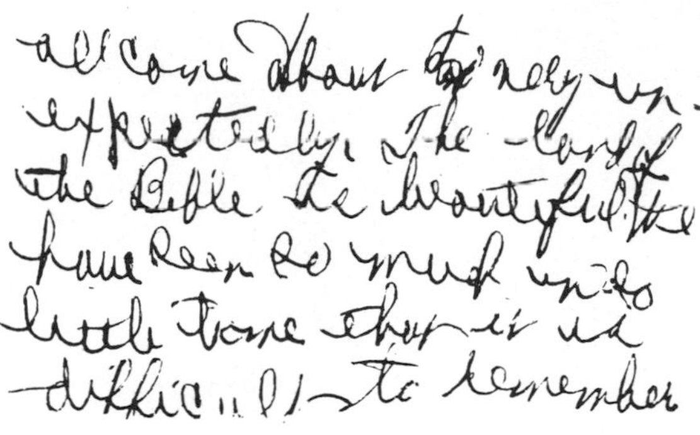

Figure 23.

Between these opposite poles, there are all kinds of changes in evenness, as well as a number of differing interpretations. As always, the Form-niveau—that is, the overall quality—of a script elicits a plus or minus diagnosis. Figure 24 shows some of the positive aspects.

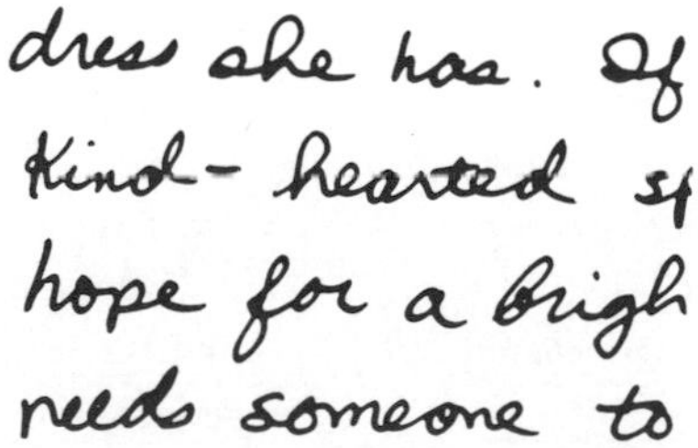

dress she has. Of
Kind- hearted s
hope for a brigh
needs someone to

Figure 24.

The writing of Figure 24 flows naturally. There is evenness without dullness. The writer is inwardly calm, and his life is well under control. Figure 25 proves that unevenness need not be devalued. Here is a lively, happy person with a somewhat high FN.

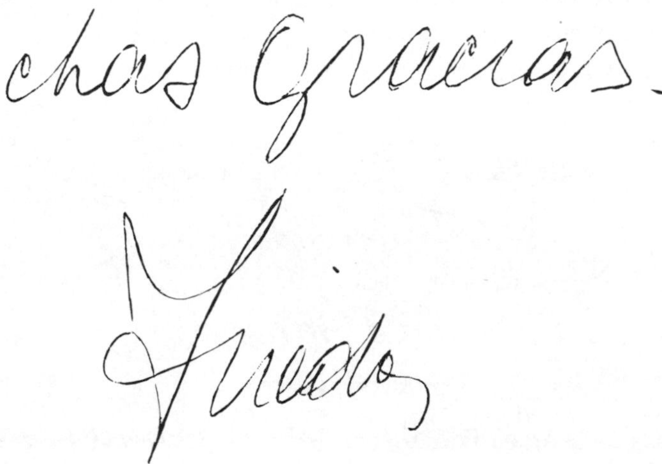

Figure 25.

Through the years, I have made notes of some traits I have encountered among the even versus the eneven writers. The accompanying table, which I developed, allows you to test your own handwriting. The plus and minus aspects are evident enough.

EVEN SCRIPT		**UNEVEN SCRIPT**	
+FN	*−FN*	*+FN*	*−FN*
Plus	**Minus**	**Plus**	**Minus**
Sticks to task	Dullness	Interesting	Changeability
Sense of order	Banality	Vivaciousness	Indecisiveness
Sense of duty	Cookie-cutter personality	Warmth, emotion	Lack of planning
Stamina		Impulsiveness	Superficiality
Intelligence		Spontaneousness	Moodiness
Tranquility			Temperamental

The Tempo

Along with a script's regularity, you will at once detect speed, or the absence of it. The latter is shown by slow, carefully executed letters and words. In fact, some writers are in the habit of writing so slowly that the point of their pen begins to tremble, which is easy to spot. On the other hand, speed is also easy to recognize because the person attempts the shortest route. Abbreviations and ingeniously connected letters are common. These connections enable the writer to pick up speed as the pen travels across the page. When the speed increases, the horizontal expansion, that is, the links between letters, will also increase. It is easier and faster to connect all the letters in a word than to lift the pen each time.

There are some other indications of fast writing. Among them:

- Simplifications and contractions
- Flattening, string-like connections
- Widening left margins, irregular right margins
- Irregularly placed i-dots and t-bars
- Tendency to become less legible

Indications of slow writing:

- Angular or arched letter forms and connections
- Precisely placed i-dots and t-bars
- Horizontal and terminal strokes come to a blunt ending or turn left
- No variation in the pressure pattern, or extra pressure

FAST SCRIPT		**SLOW SCRIPT**	
+*FN*	−*FN*	+*FN*	−*FN*
Plus	**Minus**	**Plus**	**Minus**
Energy	Haste	Self-control	Premeditation
Industry	Superficiality	Serenity	Laziness
Eagerness	Impatience	Steadiness	Apathy
Elan	Unreliability	Thoroughness	Slow learner
Enthusiasm	Moodiness		Naivete
Quick mind	Thoughtlessness		
	Easy to influence		
	Impulsiveness		

Two previous samples (Figure 4 and Figure 9) show slow penmanship. Figures 18 and 23 show penmanship of fast writers.

What does it all mean? How do you tie the tempo in to your analysis?

Once more, the Formniveau is decisive when it comes to your interpretation. The table on page 31 shows you how to evaluate slow and fast scripts. As indicated previously, the "+" means a quality writing; the "−" stands for an inferior one. Some of the above traits can easily be backed up with additional graphological findings, such as pressure, print size, and margins, all to be discussed.

The Slant

To the budding graphologist, the slant of a handwriting should become important because it reveals so much about a person's inner makeup and the emotions. Slant is most revealing. The rules are easy to grasp, and they work almost infallibly every time. In fact, once you know how to interpret the lean of a script, you will already know much about a person.

The rules of slant apply to even small samples, say two lines or so, and if you have nothing else, the signature should yield some information. Naturally, as usual, a full page or more seems desirable. You can then judge the lean at the bottom of the page, where the writer usually moves faster and more spontaneously.

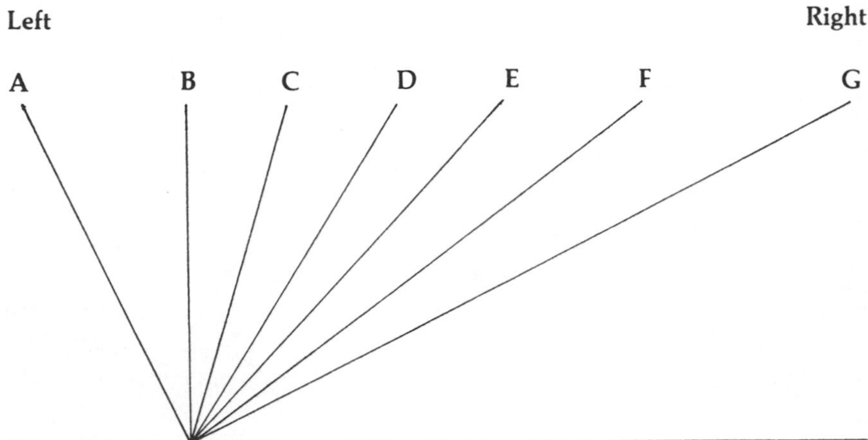

Expressed in simple terms, a writing can slope to the right or left or remain vertical.

The chart on page 32 shows seven possible angles that move from the right (G) to the left (A). As you will observe, the B-line is the vertical one.

Graphologists the world over have long agreed that the degree of slope indicates a writer's ability to feel (or show) emotions. The lean is always an indicator of possible warmth and affection. A person's temperament may range from cool (left lean) to caring (right), from basically asocial (left) to sociable and outgoing (right). Slant gives you an immediate insight into someone's ability to feel and to love (C, D, E). And you will find it easy to spot the unfeeling, introverted, or reserved individual (A).

If a handwriting leans in the direction of G, F, or E, a person will be more emotional (especially the G-type). Certainly most of the right-leaning people should be seen in a more positive light; these writers are generally more humane than those whose words slant in the opposite direction (A). Needless to say, it all depends on your own needs. If you are in search of a spouse or friend, and true affection seems important, then you should choose C, D, and E writers. Their slight slope seems ideal for persons in need of warmth. Extreme affection, and in some cases dependency, are evident in the F-line.

How about the exaggerated forward lean of line G? Here you can count on overt emotions and feelings, and, in conjunction with large lower loops, a sexually passionate person. While the F-type is capable of passion and is definitely an extrovert, the G-type can be too much so. When the words and letters nearly hug the baseline, you may be dealing with a highly charged individual. The overdone G-slant can belong to the political zealot or the sexually active (with large lower loops). If the handwriting is also fast and somewhat chaotic, there may be a lack of control.

To be sure, G-hands that head in all directions inevitably warn you that there may be a lack of stability. The confused and hysterical write in this manner, which is expressed by disjointed letters, varied pen pressures, and other graphic extremes. If you are a personnel director, and you receive an application written in a style like Figure 27 (p. 36), you must expect a somewhat wild, undisciplined, unstable person. Graphologists agree that any writing beyond the F-incline spells trouble, especially in low FN cases. The writers are too responsive to their emotions and to various stimuli. The G-group is made up of people who fly off the handle, of fanatics, and of those who refuse to consider the other side.

Conversely, C-writers control their emotions and usually have cooler heads. Indeed, the more a handwriting gravitates toward the center—in our case the B-line—the more the head rules the emotions. Completely vertical writing is often seen among brainy people who must keep their cool and control their own emotions: corporate officers, comptrollers, C.P.A.'s, attorneys, policemen, detectives and pilots. (This is not to say that all of the above write a vertical script; many of these people are miscast in their professions.)

The B-writer is known for being objective, calm and controlled. Unless the B-direction is belied by a confused, disjointed letter pattern, the writer will ponder decisions and weigh all factors. Certainly he or she is not rash. One graphologist compares the vertical hand to "a person standing erect, someone who cannot be swayed one way or another." Keep in mind that if a vertical writer has a flowing, round handwriting, there is warmth, too, although she may not carry her heart on her sleeve. Round handwriting, whether of the genre B, C, or D, always belongs to people who can adapt. (One caveat—the writing should not change directions; it must stick to one slant.)

A total left lean, as in A, is the other extreme, of course.

The more a writing tips to the left, the more reserved and unapproachable is the person. A-writers are always introverted, often unfeeling, and, in a few cases, when the capitals are separate from the rest of the word, possibly hermits or recluses. Even if they feel, A-writers cannot *demonstrate* warmth or love on the surface. The communication of good feelings is vital to relationships, of course. On the other hand, the lack of warmth or capacity to sympathize hardly matters if you are trying to hire a janitor or C.P.A. If the A-writer has an orderly, organized script, he or she deserves the job, and will probably do it well. The left slant indicates a withdrawal tendency; the writer can be lively and vivacious, but basically self-centered. If the writers are mature adults they usually have experienced some unpleasantness within themselves.

Some hands come, not only with an extreme left slant, but also with all kinds of angles and an absence of loops. Such a person is likely to be a cold fish indeed; if the A-writer also exhibits sharp points, hooks, and daggers, you will be faced with a malicious, unpleasant individual, especially if the letters seem to be at all angles. Dr. Max Pulver discovered that exaggerated A-writers, especially those with angular formations, are often psychopaths. Pulver's theory is borne out by the handwriting of a well-known female gun slinger of the Wild West, whose script was full of angles, and also tipped completely to the left (see Figure 50), on page 55.

Men and women whose hand leans backward do so, Dr. Pulver tells us, for symbolic reasons. They are turning away, withdrawing emotionally, or curtailing their emotions. To be sure, the backhand pen-wielder cannot be seduced with any ease. Such a person resists all persuasiveness of others. The A-line is a sign of caution, a refusal to reach out (as the C-D-E writer does), and self-protection. The Swiss graphologist also came to the conclusion that the backhand writer gave graphic evidence of aloofness. The extreme left lean does not allow for a genuine naturalness. Such writers, I find, are generally uptight and closed, especially if their m's and n's are closed on top and look like arches, and if the O's (and o's) contain spiderweb patterns of a circular nature.

Every graphologist will admit that a high Formniveau—the truly genial writing of a high caliber—reverses some of the effects of the exaggerated A-lean. A superior hand demands a fresh and more positive interpretation. In my estimation, the A-writer with an FN 5 or FN 4 possesses a sense of tact. He or she uses restraint and prizes self-control. True aristocrats and diplomats write this way, and you can almost be sure that Protocol Chiefs, the people who teach diplomats about etiquette, can be superior A-writers, if not B's or C's.

What if the handwriting moves in *different* directions? The situation in that case is an intriguing one.

The crucial question is age. The wavering script may well be that of a youth struggling with puberty. The temporary troubles of growing up, with all its moods and the strains of oncoming sexuality, express themselves in a constantly changing slant. (Teenagers should not be judged too harshly if they exhibit a strong backward lean. The A-line may be due to suppressed sexuality or prudence.)

In an adult, frequent direction changes generally point to a change of moods. If the words waver from left to right and right to left and the handwriting is thin and without pressure, you are in the presence of one who is not only moody but also indecisive and vacillating. Lack of inner strength, confusion, capriciousness, or simple fatigue also show up through such changes. It is wise to ask for (and study) several handwriting samples of the same person, written over a period of days, or better, weeks. The changes of direction may be a temporary one, indicating a struggle with a temporary problem. When it is solved,the slant will be back to normal. On the other hand, chronic slant-shifting, especially if the lines waver and if there are severe disturbances in rhythm, reveal writers whose stability is questionable. They make unreliable mates.

In a normally C- or D-slanted script, there may be a sudden tendency to shift to B (or even A) at the ends of words or lines. This means the writer is basically warm, but makes a great effort to use self-control and caution.

Slant remains one of the most graphic and easy-to-detect tools. The following illustrations will show you some typical slant samples and their analysis.

Thanks.

Figure 26. The vertical hand; the B-slant. Clearheaded, intelligent, and practical—the latter two qualities shown also by the simplified letters. Capitals contain only the essentials, a good sign for intelligence.

Figure 27. Inconstant lean, with tendency to topple to the right, denotes impulsiveness, changeability. The illegible writing points to an inconsiderate person-who does not care if you can read the message or not. A bad sign.

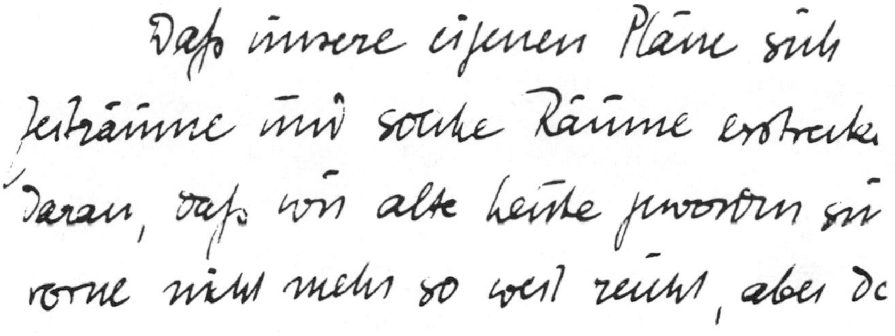

Figure 28. Intelligent, tactful, high-caliber penmanship, with much balance and interesting capitals. The lean indicates a capacity for affection.

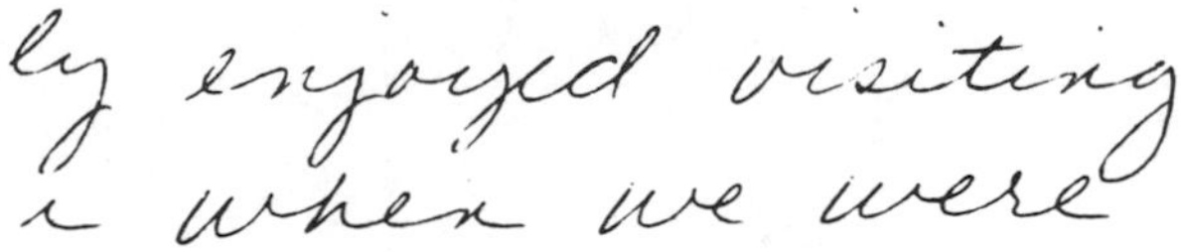

Figure 29. There is warmth here and other positive character traits, such as stability, loyalty, and a basic purity. The writing contains no artifice, no deviation, no change in size. A dependable person.

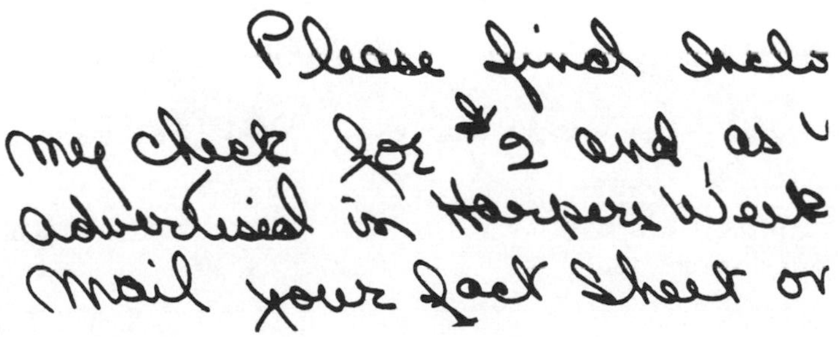

Figure 30. Too much backhand (line A). A very reserved individual, also corroborated by the arc-like, secretive m's and n's.

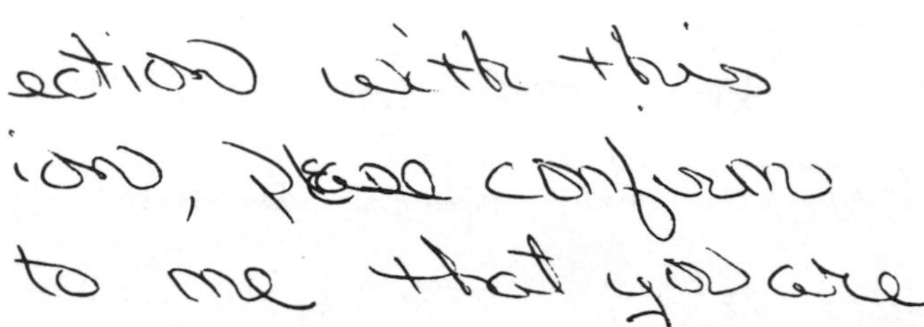

Figure 31. Another backhand style, A-line. This one even slower, denoting a cramped attitude toward others. The arches and sharp points typify an adult with asocial tendencies.

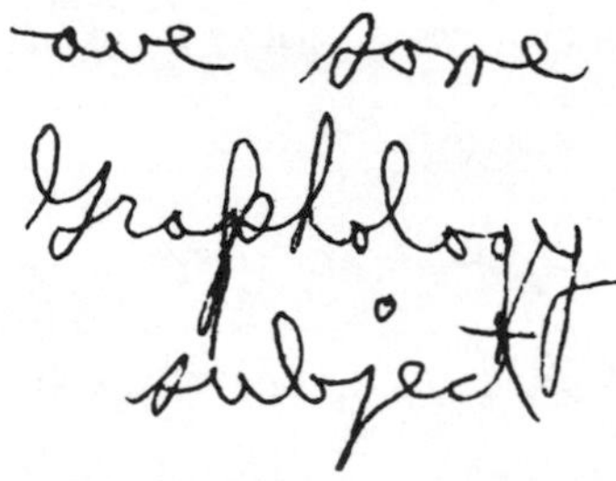

Figure 32. Adult male with frequent direction changes. Moodiness can be confirmed by various other samples of the same male, written over the period of a year.

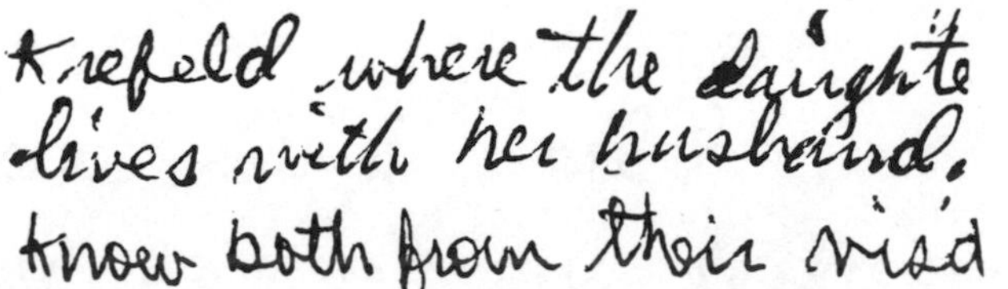

Krefeld where the daughte
lives with her husband.
know both from their visit

Figure 33. Sixteen-year-old boy with frequent slant shifts, indicating puberty and normal growth problems.

The table below by Felix Klein amplifies some of the interpretations of a right slant (upper portion of letters tipping to right) or left slant (top portion of t's, among others, tip to left). Reading down, traits are from a slight to an extreme slant, with the latter appearing at the bottom of the lists.

RIGHT SLANT		LEFT SLANT	
+FN	*−FN*	*+FN*	*−FN*
Plus	**Minus**	**Plus**	**Minus**
Readiness to say yes	Subjective feelings	Restraint	Coolness
Humaneness (contact)	Emphasis on impulses	Independence	Cannot be moved
Responsiveness	Extravagance	Attempt to remain strong	Inhibition
Compliance	Dependency		Not responsive
Geniality	Says yes to everything		Aloofness
Passion	Lack of distance		Unkind person
	Gullibility		

Handwriting Size

The size of a handwriting is another important clue to a personality. It shows how one views oneself, and it tells something about self-confidence, pride, poise, or the lack of these. In conjunction with width, size can reveal traits like generosity or miserliness; in combination with the amount of pressure of the pen on the paper, size gives the graphologist an idea about one's enthusiasm or restraint, or one's vitality or the absence of it. As always, the Formniveau enters into play. A small script in a superior handwriting must be interpreted differently from the small hand in the sloppy, slapdash style.

How does the graphologist determine what is small and what is large?

Some specimens, like those in Figures 34 and 35, clearly reveal the enormous and the tiny script.

Others fall somewhere in between. A typical North American elementary school teacher would tell us that the middle zone letters like the a's should measure about one-eighth of an inch or from 2.5 to 3.5

Figure 34.

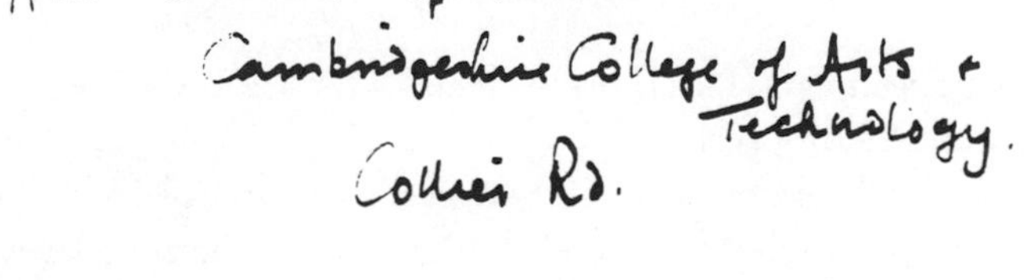

Asst. Director of Music
Cambridgeshire College of Arts & Technology.
Collier Rd.

Figure 35.

millimeters. In Europe, the average is about 3 millimeters.) The width between the arches of the letters h, m, and n are as wide as their height. The proportion of the upper loops on letters with extensions are 1½ times as tall as the middle zone letters. Lower loops, such as the g and the y, are generally twice as long as the e's and i's. The distance between the letters is about one-sixteenth of an inch, and between words measures about one-eighth of an inch in width. The capitals achieve the same height as the upper zones. The only exception to the above is the top of the d. It is slightly shorter than the upper zone of the lower case h, l, f, and k.

All these measurements are only approximations because some schools teach children slightly different ratios and sizes. Dr. Pulver once explained that an adult's departure from the school norm shows independent thought and creativity; by the same token, wildly exaggerated graphic inventions indicate an immature individual. One could add, of course, that graphic extremes in the size of handwriting, such as the huge "John" in Figure 34, diminish overall quality and decrease the Formniveau. By contrast, even the dainty English sample in Figure 35 deserves a good rating; its rhythm, speed, consistency, and harmony are all above average. The writer is a noted British choral conductor and musicologist.

In combination with a variety of graphological signs, and depending on a person's background, education, and other particulars, size can point to a number of possibilities.

LARGE SCRIPT		**SMALL SCRIPT**	
+FN	*−FN*	*+FN*	*−FN*
Plus	**Minus**	**Plus**	**Minus**
Enthusiasm	Exaltation	Realism	Lack of enthusiasm
Initiative	Lack of control	Thoroughness	Little vitality
Generosity	Superficiality	Scientific bent	Timidity
Pride	Spendthrift	Considerateness	Pettiness
Action	Conceit	Ability to concentrate	Miserliness
Joie de vivre	Impulsiveness	Humility	Fear (cowardice)
	Pompousness		Inferiority complex

At this juncture, it would be wise to look at some actual examples delineating the writers' personalities and determine if the script is large or small.

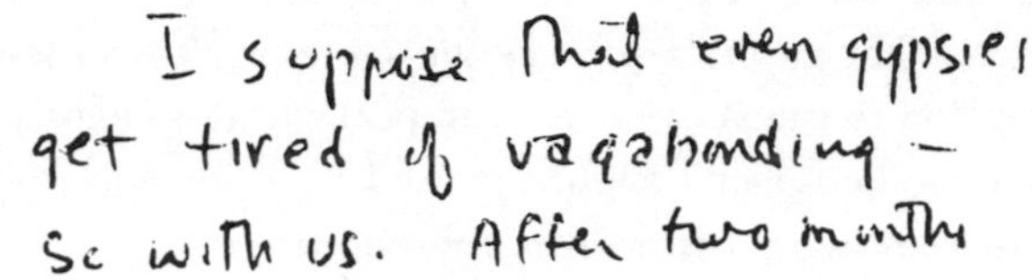

Figure 36.

Small, precise, well-formed letters, as in Figure 36, show an ability to concentrate, to examine a problem critically without being influenced by outward distractions. As a high school principal, this man's attention to detail makes him well suited for research, which he does independently. Note that the small and legible script is upright, indicating control over his emotions. The writer fills the space with an eye for aesthetics and organization. His capitals (see the "A") and word formations ("that" in line 1) are original. All this places the writer into a high-caliber Formniveau (FN 5).

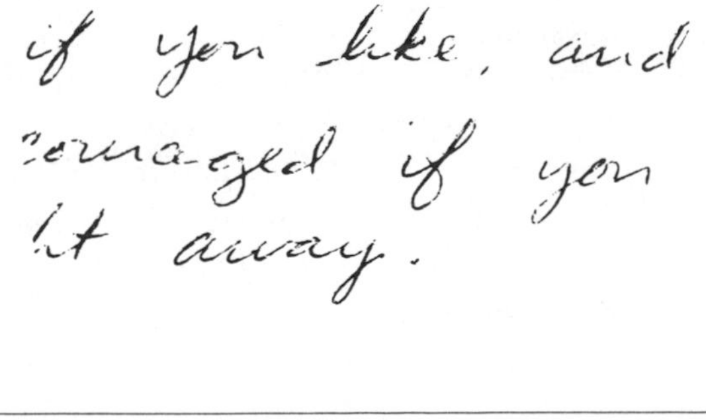

Figure 37.

In Figure 37 the writing is slightly larger than that of the school official and the previously shown musicologist, but it should still be considered small. The Formniveau is good, thanks to the lack of adornment and the flow of the writing. The combination shows a young woman who is able to concentrate. She is a librarian and well-regarded by her superiors. The size of her script indicates attention to detail, one of her qualifications for the library job.

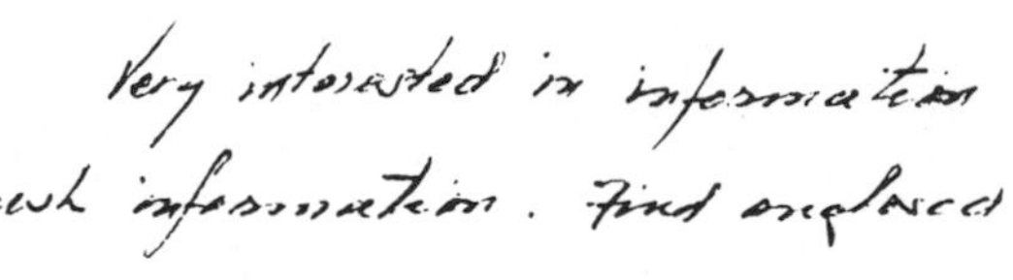

Figure 38.

The small writing in Figure 38 lacks rhythm and motion; the writer "brakes" almost constantly. His hesitation, the many pauses with carefully arched "m's" and "n's" and the inward-turning word endings (see the "d" in "Find") are those of a shy, unsure, fearful individual. The writing almost ducks; there is very little self-esteem here.

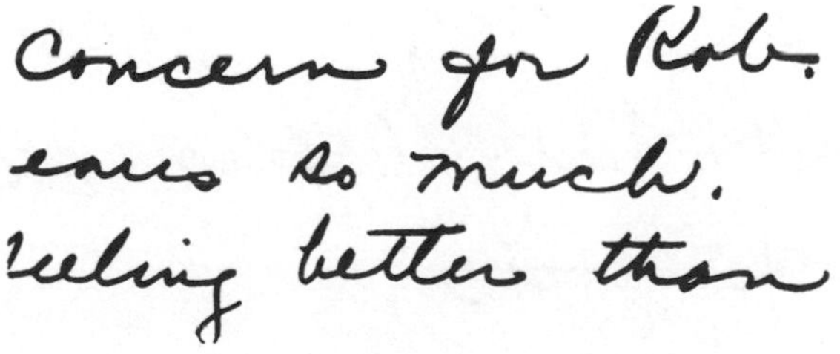

Figure 39.

Figure 39 should be termed a medium-sized handwriting; apart from its average American size, it is rhythmic and pleasantly flowing. The ends of the words, unlike those of Figure 38 reach out boldly and warmly. The woman who wrote the sample in Figure 39 knows where she is going and where she stands, and is not intimidated by others.

Figure 40.

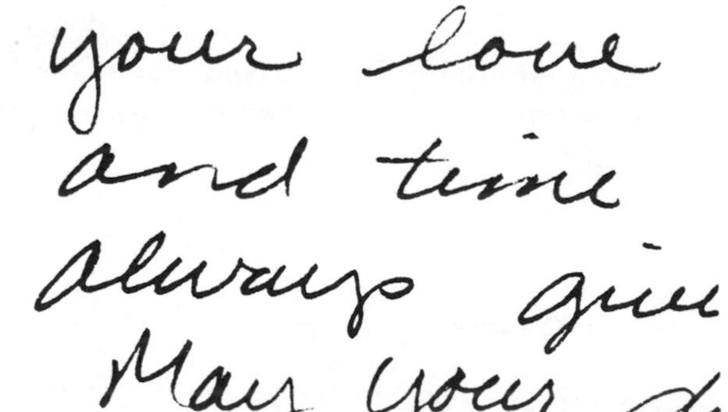

Figure 41.

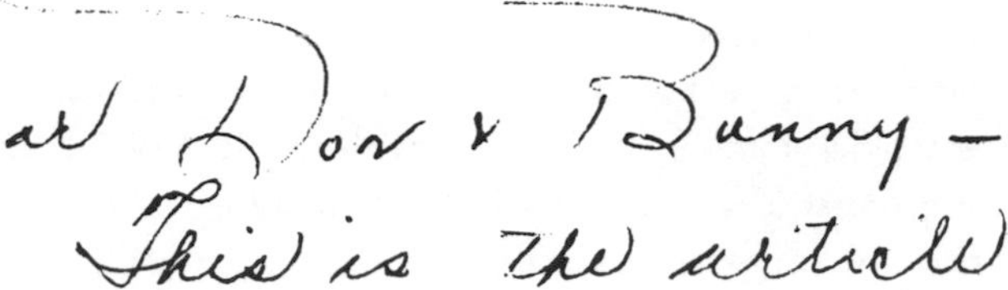

Figure 42.

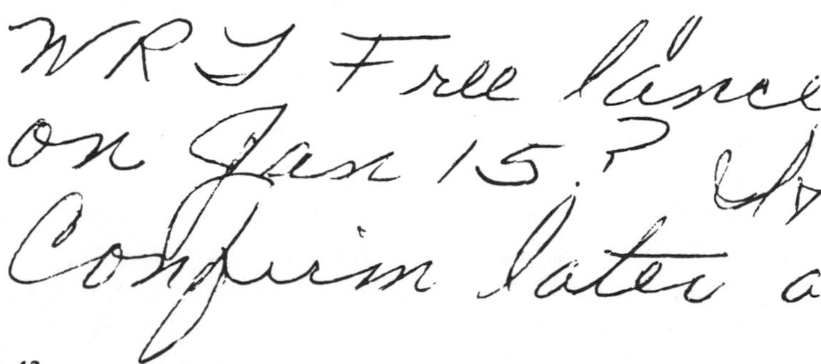

Figure 43.

Figures 40, 41, 42, and 43 all illustrate the large hand. The capital "M" in Figure 40, which belongs to a wealthy society matron, has a particular elegance and pride; according to some of Dr. Pulver's research, the descending portions of the M should be interpreted in a positive light. Here is a woman who is willing to come to the aid of others. Figure 41 also shows large handwriting, but the script sways in one direction and then another, which, as we have learned, always signals moodiness, capriciousness, and, in this case, a somewhat spendthrift nature.

The Large Hands

Two additional samples will delve into other interpretations of the large hand. In Figure 42, only the capitals are oversized, especially the "D" in "Don" and the "B" in "Bunny." Overblown capitals such as these in a writing that is somewhat small and downright conventional always warn of conceit; a modest person creates modest capitals. The unnecessary flourishes show a trend toward bragging or showing off.

When the size reaches that shown in Figure 34, rendered in its original size, we must suspect arrogance; in connection with the backward slant, the writing loses some of its human qualities. It is of a stand-offish, basically arrogant person who will push others around.

The writer of large letters, as shown in Figure 43, may be the conceiver of grand plans. She shuns the mundane and sees herself as being a bit larger than life. She does not necessarily consider herself to be superior to those around her, but she knows her abilities. Large writing is frequently employed by those who seek the admiration and the adulation of others.

The Three Zones and What They Mean

The discussion of a script's size leads logically to the proportions of upper, middle, and lower zones, and to their meanings.

Handwriting is divided into three zones. The upper zone is occupied by letters b, d, f, h, k, and l, as well as the i-dot and the t-bar.

The middle zone includes the letters a, c, e, i, m, n, o, r, s, u, v, w, and x, and the bodies of the b, d, f, g, h, j, k, p, q, y, and z.

The lower zone is in the lower extensions of letters f, q, j, p, g, y, and z.

The American writing system teaches that the middle zone should measure one-eighth of an inch. The upper extensions achieve about 1½ times the height of the middle zone, and the lower zone is 1½ times as long as the height of the middle zone.

After leaving school, many writers no longer maintain these proportions, but create their own, discarding copybook letter sizes, slants and margins. Dr. Max Pulver, who introduced symbolism during the 1930's, observed that man looks up to the heavens (and religion), the stars, the spirit, and the human mind. All these fall into the upper zones of our writing. The lower zone is earthy in character; here are our roots and instincts, the material sphere. The amount of space we allot to the three zones reveals much about our reaction to the world around us.

Here are the capabilities of Homo sapiens that distinguish us from animals; that is, our idealism and our sense of reality as well as our materialism. Here is man's intellect (upper zone), sexual drive (lower zone), pursuit of ideals (upper), and quest for money (lower). The zones, Dr.

Pulver once said (with Freud's approval), may well point to the super ego (upper), the ego (middle), and the id (lower).

As always, the Formniveau matters greatly. For example, a long, elegantly swung lower loop can indicate a solid business talent, but if the loop is coarse and ill-formed in an inferior writing, the person may be merely money-grasping. (A balance in all three zones always signifies maturity in an otherwise acceptable FN.)

Let's examine some other specific possibilities.

An emphasis on the upper zone is often found in mystics, in the devoutly religious, in the patriotic, and in the idealistic. (The handwriting in Figure 20 may be typical of this in its emphasis on the upper zone. Its braininess is indicated by the erect posture, with a strong sense of idealism.) The handwritings of mystics and passionately religious people would lean more, and would show greater graphic extremes.

Most graphologists also mention, correctly, that a larger upper zone development always applies to mentally agile people, especially in fast handwriting. Certainly you can be sure that a long h extension (and other extensions) belongs to the abstract thinker, or the person with a bent toward philosophy or spirituality.

Swooping high toward the sky, especially in the upper part of the d (written like a musical note) can be an indication of lofty goals and lack of interest in the mundane and trivial. A large, round script with exaggerated capitals may show ambition; in a disorganized script, we may be dealing with a daydreamer, or a person who is mainly interested in theory and not in action. (Corroboration for this can be found in the lack of pen pressure.) This writer's head may be in the clouds, especially if the writing does not seem to have much vitality or strength (vitality means above average size or pressure). An exaggerated upper zone of the letters and capitals, with simplified A's, B's, and other formations, generally suggests the intellectual.

How about a very small upper zone? In a low FN, the lack of normal extensions means that the writer lacks a probing, truly interested mind; if the lower zones, by contrast, are overblown, the missing upper dimension denotes an absence of spiritual qualities and ideals. This conclusion can be backed by a coarse writing, along with the stunted spiritual life.

The area below the baseline has to do with our libido and with material drives; here are our instincts and the satisfaction of our senses. Depending on the FN, the strokes, and the nature of the loops, the lower zone and its emphasis (or absence of it) has to do with our enjoyment of sex, good food, and music as well as with sports and material aspirations. In a rounded, muddy, heavy, pasty writing, good living is underlined by a well-developed lower zone. The latter indicates sports in large, strong, disciplined, and rhythmic hands.

What if the lower zone is badly developed? The g's (and other such letters) may be short and come without loops, indicating a person whose earthly roots are precarious. Such people show little interest in the good things of life; unless they have ideals or an intellect (high upper extensions), the short, no-loop g-types can be easily uprooted; they cannot hang on in the face of calamity. An underdeveloped lower zone can signify lack of sexual interest, sexual immaturity; the writers seldom go for athletics or other physical pursuits. According to Felix Klein, the neglect of the lower zone can also imply a lack of depth.

Writing that is conspicuously heavy below the baseline, with weak upper structures, discloses an elemental nature, with strong instincts and passions. Some previous illustrations (Figure 28 and Figure 10 respectively) show lack of libido, especially Figure 10. A strongly sexed person's handwriting appears in Figure 44 below. (Note large loops.)

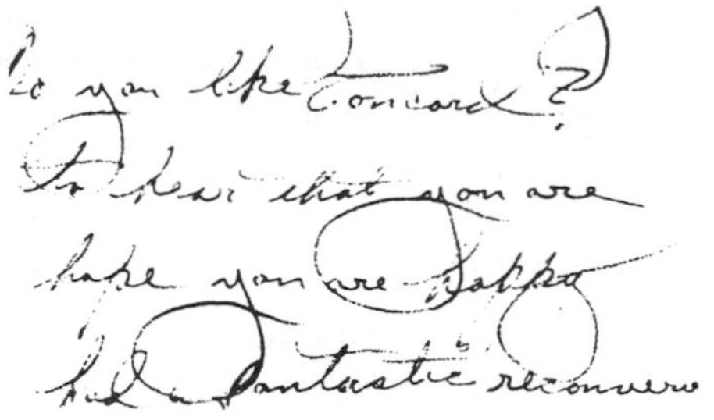

Figure 44.

By definition, a loop is any enclosure formed by two strokes that touch or intersect. They may fall into any area of a word, as shown by upper zone loops, middle zone loops, and lower zone loops.

A loop simply reveals the extent of the writer's imagination in that particular area. As a rule, the greater the width of the loop, the greater the imagination; the narrower the loop, the smaller the interest. The especially large loops in the lower extensions, like Figure 44, are those of sensualists; in the upper part of a script (such as the "l") you will find the people with imagination.

Naturally, anything can be overdone. If the upper loop is nearly three times the average width, it means that the individual allows his imagination to run away. (This can be useful to a novelist.) Flights of fantasy can be suspected if the giant loops occur in a low Formniveau. A high FN with narrow loops points to a limited imagination, but also an ability to look at all aspects of a problem, that is, objectivity.

There remains one zone to be discussed. It is the middle, or central zone. It has to do with the practical aspects of someone's life. The mundane shows up here, and you can deduce a person's viewpoints. "The middle zone, symbolic of the present, will determine to what degree we carry out our daily routine, how well we cooperate with others. The middle zone means the present," explains one of my colleagues.

If the middle zone is extra large and the upper and lower ones appear neglected, you are dealing with a basically realistic, down-to-earth person. Religion assumes as little importance in his or her daily life as physical pursuits, as in Figure 45, for example.

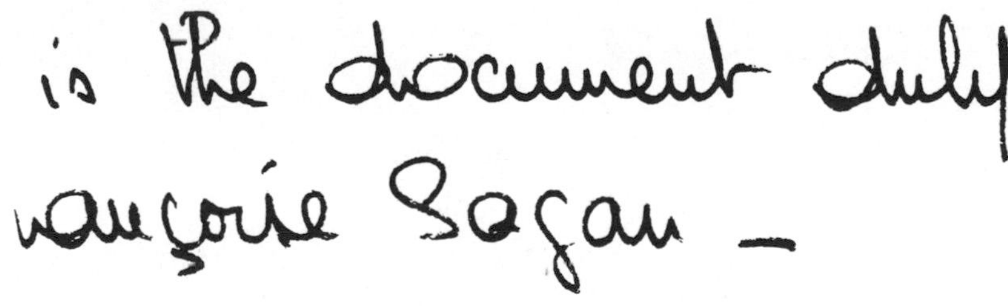

Figure 45.

The strong middle zone in this French script shows a capable woman editor (also underlined by the erect slant) who believes in doing her job. Neither "y" nor "g" emphasizes sexual interest.

Oversized middle zones also appear at times in the hands of young people (Figure 15 on page 22). If the FN is as high as this one, you can be sure that the young person does well in school and in life, even if some other areas must be neglected a bit, for a time. The exceptionally handsome writing of Figure 15 points to great intelligence and practicality; this happens to be the script of a female law student. In lesser scripts (see Figure 6 on page 7) you can suspect a slow maturing; the youth is still uninterested in sex or intellect. In a rounded writing, an over-large middle zone expresses good-humored naivete.

What would be the ideal zonal situation? You might call it "zonal balance."

Look at Figure 9 (on page 16). There are several words with branches into both upper and lower zones. Notice that the script is fairly well divided among all three zones. The loops are neither skimpy nor overblown. This indicates that the writer is well-balanced. He is in touch with reality, baseline in the middle zone; he has the capacity for abstract thought, as shown by the upper zone extensions; and he is aware of his physical and instinctual needs, as shown by his lower zone extensions.

3

More Essentials

We have seen that the graphologist is guided by specifics in the handwriting, which include the slant, the size, and the use of upper, middle, and lower zones. All these convey different meanings in an uneven or even writing, or one with a high or low Formniveau; that is, script quality.

Width and Narrowness

The width of someone's strokes, words, and lines also gives some clues to character and mentality, just as the use of space (between words and between lines) becomes important, along with margins of all kinds. Besides width, this chapter will also explore other such essentials as connections of letters, pressure, and the motion of a writing. Along the route, it may be worth your while to reread some of the earlier material, so that you are ready to absorb more data. As you progress, keep in mind that every new graphological rule works only in relationship to the remainder of a writing.

This is also true for the width between letters.

If a handwriting is wide, with wide connections between letters, the verdict would be that the writer is eager to communicate, working hard to reach the right margin. This is true for a satisfactory or better-than-average script quality. However, if the wide connections occur in a low Formniveau, the width merely indicates haste and impatience. In an especially harsh-looking script, with too much pressure and a low FN, the width applies to people who "elbow" others; that is, the pushy persons.

In a large, warm, rounded, leaning hand (as written by an affable, affectionate individual), the extra width expresses generosity. (See figure 46 below.)

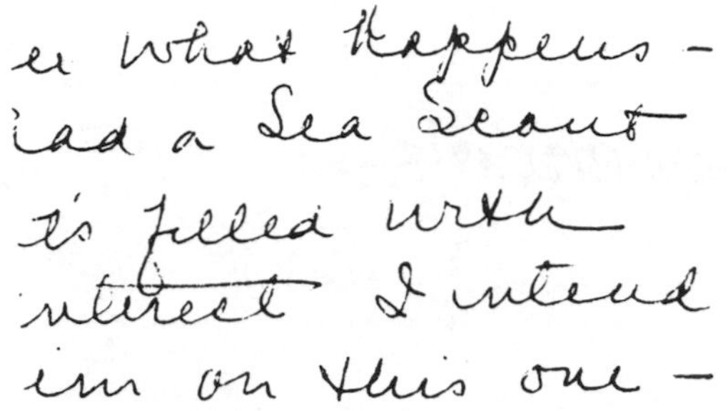

Figure 46.

Figure 47 indicates generosity. The writing not only is extra wide for its size, but also the letters "n" and "m" are open, "garland"-style, and there is a pleasant roundness about all the strokes. The erect posture merely shows that the writer thinks before she acts, or bestows gifts.

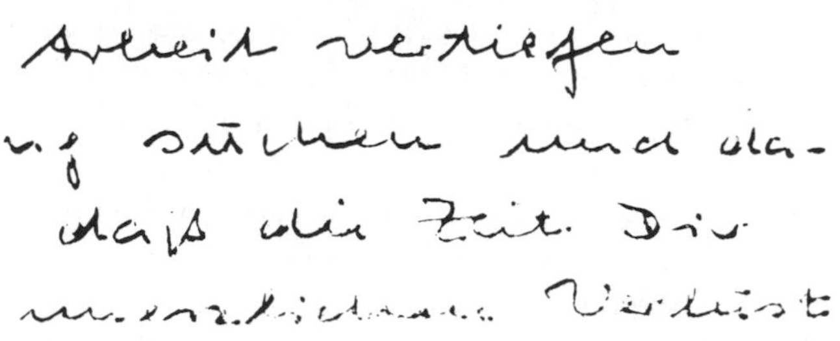

Figure 47.

Her speed indicates a naturalness, which is a pleasant trait indeed. By contrast, slow writers who so adorn their letters can seldom be natural. For an example of such script, study Figure 48. The writing is wide enough, but it is contrived and written slowly, with a backhand slant. Here is a person who wants to appear generous, but is in reality very cautious.

Figure 48.

Figure 49.

How about "tight" writers? What do they want to express by their letters close together? Why do they write this way? There may be several reasons. If the narrowness is found in a well-done FN (Figure 49), self-control and tact are at work; the writer merely holds back. Tightness, along with nonexistent (or narrow) margins, means extreme thrift. In a negative script, however, the meaning changes altogether and points to fearful, distrustful writers, or, in backhand scripts, to those who lack warmth. This is summed up in the following table.

WIDE SCRIPT		NARROW SCRIPT	
+FN	*−FN*	*+FN*	*−FN*
Plus	**Minus**	**Plus**	**Minus**
Naturalness	Hastiness	Self-control	Fear
Generosity	Impatience	Tact	Lack of warmth
Need for space	Elbowing	Thrift	Distrust
Hard worker			

Connections and Disconnections

Just as size, slant, and zones are indicators of human characteristics, so do connections add a new dimension to the analysis. We have already mentioned wide or tight connections; logically, we can also draw conclusions from connections with the following:

Sharp angles
Extremely round strokes
Certain open letters, known as garlands
Closed letters, known as arcades
Formations that look like mere threads
Absence of connections (disconnected letters)

Let's look at all these possibilities, one by one.

Roundness Versus Angularity

If a handwriting has many sharp angular connections, it can mean several things, depending on the overall quality. The following table will introduce you to the meanings of angularity and roundness.

ANGULAR SCRIPT		**ROUND SCRIPT**	
+FN	*−FN*	*+FN*	*−FN*
Plus	**Minus**	**Plus**	**Minus**
Strength	Rigidity	Accommodating	Naive
Critical faculties	Nastiness	Warm, good humored	
Objectivity	Dry	Adaptable	
Tenacity	Inability to yield	Easy going	

The only exception to the above rule on angularity is scripts of people who were educated in Germany. The *Deutsche* schools, especially prior to World War II, taught an angular Gothic style which can be hard to discard, even for German-Americans. Likewise, for Americans born in Russia, the many angles that appear in the Russian alphabet should be taken into account. The sharpness often persists when such a person becomes a United States citizen. The above explains why extreme angles are a telltale phenomenon when found in North American writers.

Two such specimens appear below.

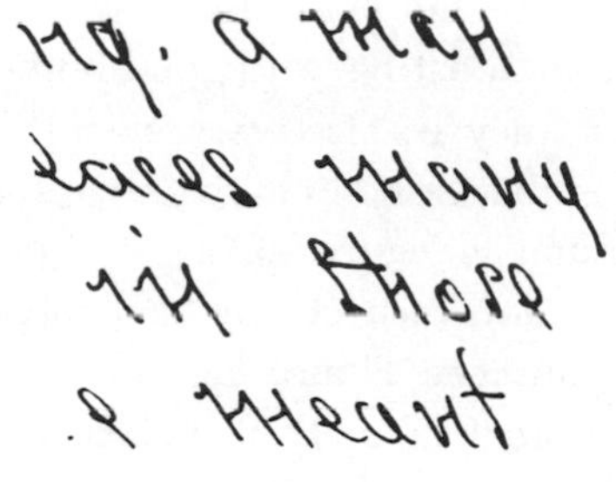

Figure 50.

Figure 51.

Both are interesting. Figure 50 happens to be the thorny, premeditated, almost brutally angular writing of Ann Bassett, a lady gun slinger of the old Wild West, well-known for her nastiness toward people she did not like. The specimen in Figure 51 belongs to a more impulsive but cynical man, whose sharp connections reveal a nagging man who is hard to live with.

By contrast, Figure 28 identifies a well-known West German painter and art professor with outstanding critical faculties. His FN is superb. Similarly, certain angles in the American script in Figure 14 show a discriminating woman whose high FN speaks of good taste.

In angular writing it is necessary to momentarily stop at the point where the angles are formed; therefore, angular writing is never fast writing. Round connections have the opposite connotation. Round letters can be written faster. In fact, if one's handwriting is harmonious and well-balanced, as well as original, such round links show a fine sense of adapting to others. One moves along smoothly, trying to overcome obstacles, not through brute, angular force, but by means of waves. Such "round" writers are generally kind, accommodating, and good-humored. If their script has an affectionate lean to it, they are also warm people. How about the roundness in an inferior FN? In that case, you are face to face with a naive person.

One previous example, Figure 45, shows a pleasant individual. This French woman editor is highly respected in her profession, partly because of her gracious way with authors. Figure 52, below, also emphasizes round links. The few small angles in this well-balanced script suggest a sophisticated individual.

Figure 52.

The Arcade Writer

Most writers deviate from the connective style they were taught in their early penmanship days. After all, handwriting is a true reflection of one's inner self, and the formations first acquired in grade school may not reflect these characteristics. For example, children had to connect each letter to the next with a smooth, curved stroke. The m's and n's came with well-rounded arcs and the letters had to be in exact proportion. The Roman arches seemed forced to some students. Maturity brought with it an individual writing style which fit them better than the copybook script they were originally taught. This breaking away from tradition is always of interest to the graphologist, especially when it comes to stroke or letter connections.

One of the prime examples of breaking out of the mold is the arcade, because it was often taught in U.S. schools. (See Figure 30, where the "m's" and "n's" are made to look like arches.) Many students soon veer off to garlands instead; that is, to open letters, as in Figures 45 and 46.

The arcade resembles a Roman arch. It can appear in superior scripts that look extremely artistic, as in the case of architects, decorators, and so on. In such well-balanced, high-quality writings, the Roman m's and n's should be seen in a positive light; the writer strives for artistry. But you will also encounter the arcade in a low to middling FN. The roof-like formation then points to the enclosed, secretive person who does not volunteer much information. The clue is of prime importance when you want to begin a relationship with someone who will open up quickly, and who is eager to communicate his or her thoughts. This is not the case with arcade writers, who favor privacy and private inner spaces, and put up a guard against others.

Certainly the arcade is a sign of the reserved individual, particularly when you encounter these m's in backhand scripts. (Quite often the person may have become cautious through certain experiences in life.)

The arch can also be found in young children and the early teens; girls of thirteen or fourteen customarily will not use open m's or n's; if they do, you can be sure of great maturity. In general, arcade types are not yet willing to reveal their inner life to anyone. Certainly, young "arcade" females will not share personal matters with their boyfriends and often withhold information from their parents.

In a mature, high-caliber script, the same reticence, however, assumes value; the arcade writer is the one who can keep secrets, and on whose discretion you can count. Indeed, in a first-rate FN such as in Figure 15, that of a young female law student, the slightly arched "m's" and "n's" point to positive traits like tact and a sense of etiquette. In a pleasant script like that of Figure 53 (on page 58), you can be sure of someone with good manners and a measure of self-control. In this case, the writer is a 49-year-old nurse whose m's still hark back to her school days.

The FN is above average, and the nurse is simply a person who likes to stick to social conventions. Older arcade writers with less harmonious graphics employ arcades to register caution or prudence. Such people have trouble opening up to their friends or lovers. If the arcade in a mature but low FN-type also leans to the backhand side, the writer is probably inscrutable

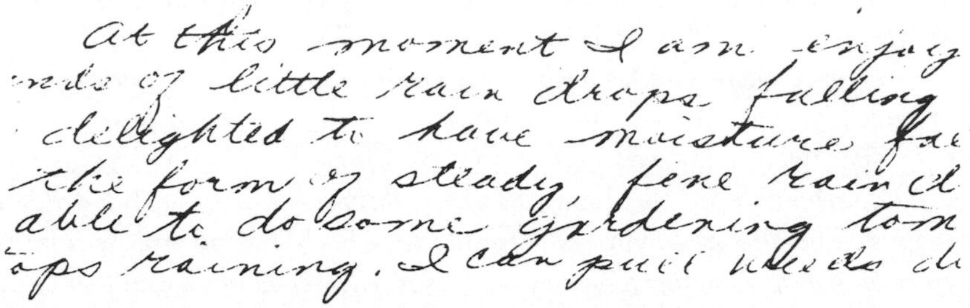

Figure 53.

as well. Abrupt endings also add a note of fear, of distrust toward others.

A few people employ arcades at the end of their signature, like an extra wall against the world. Such convex or concave cross-bars mean that the individual wants to be left alone. Some handwriting samples will present not only enormous arcades (like that in the naive example in Figure 54), but also claw-like word endings that go inward in a cramped fashion (see the ending of the word "I'm"). In a writing that is slow as well, and lacks finesse, such arcades with claws should be interpreted as asocial tendencies; in this case, a young woman who could not communicate with anyone, including her mother.

Figure 54.

Young girls, especially those who were brought up and live in small towns, often write slowly and carefully; their arcades show prudence. In a low-grade writing this caution can become grotesque and attitudes cramped. Such writers cannot be themselves; they are not natural or free, but, like the specimen in Figure 54, closed. Here there is repression, fear of contact, and even a holding back of instincts.

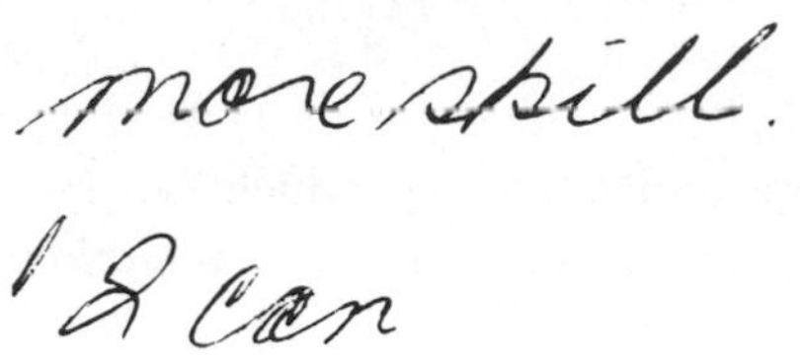

Figure 55.

Incidentally, when you spot an arcade writer who also offers spider-web-like closures of a's and o's, like those in Figure 55, you see someone who does not want her private life invaded or analyzed. Such closures confirm secretiveness and a fear of intimacy. The writer who presents us with such connections simply does not want anyone to come too close. You can be sure that his or her conversation will be superficial; and direct questions will be parried. You may even be accused of prying, even after a long acquaintance. The low-FN arcade and spiderweb writer will not give any clue to his or her real feelings, or the possibility of loneliness.

All in all, the arcade formation is a valuable tool in your evaluation. So is the garland, of course.

Garlands

The garland is the exact opposite of the arcade.

The garland m or n is open. Dr. Pulver compared it to "a vessel which is ready to receive—." The writer is more open, frank, and more ready to communicate and level with you—more apt to receive your input. The garland thus becomes a more positive sign than the secretive arcade. After all, openness is an admirable trait, especially among the young generations who do not feel that they must conceal their true feelings, like the Victorians.

The garland person can be found at all age levels. If such open letters already appear in young adults, you can be sure of maturity; they have nothing to hide. The garland-type can say "I feel bad today" or "I feel great." Garland people possess a readiness to oblige, a benevolence toward others. These persons do not like irritation or conflict. They seek smooth social relationships, and have an innate wish to get along with others. (Figures 45 and 46 are typical of this type.

Garland-types, unless you discover signs to the contrary, usually give in more easily if the other person is right. Moreover, they are more humane and more understanding, which can indeed be useful traits for anyone, especially psychologists and social workers (see Figure 56).

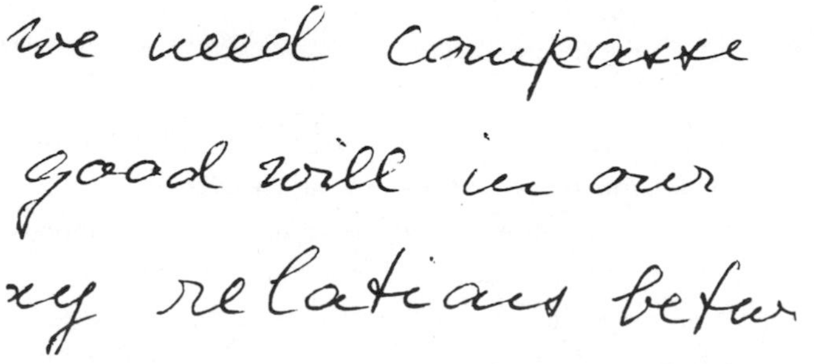

Figure 56.

Figure 56 shows a woman of 50 or so who has sympathy for others. She also has drive, balance, naturalness, strength, and taste. She is no game player. Totally honest, with an engaging simplicity, clarity, and sincerity, this woman is not a pushover. (Nor will she force her friendship on anyone.) The majority of the words are heading toward the right margin, which means that she enjoys contact with others and likes many people.

How about the garland in a low-caliber script? If it is very cramped and tight, the writer is probably shy.

In an inferior writing the garland that constantly shifts directions can also indicate gabbing, weakness, and superficiality. Figure 57 provides an example.

Figure 57 provides a mixture, a little bit of an arcade and a garland,

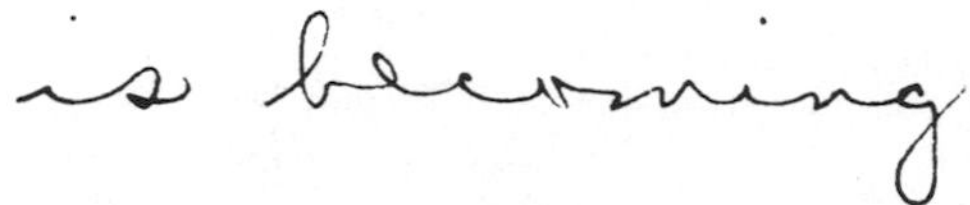

Figure 57.

an in-between case. A colleague of mine wrote: "In some scripts it is difficult to tell if it is arcade or garland, as the arcade can be pressed down to resemble a garland. The best method I have found is to trace the writing with the ballpoint pen with the point retracted. If the movement is in a counterclockwise direction, it is a garland . . . if in a clockwise direction, it is an arcade."

A few more examples will sum up what we have learned.

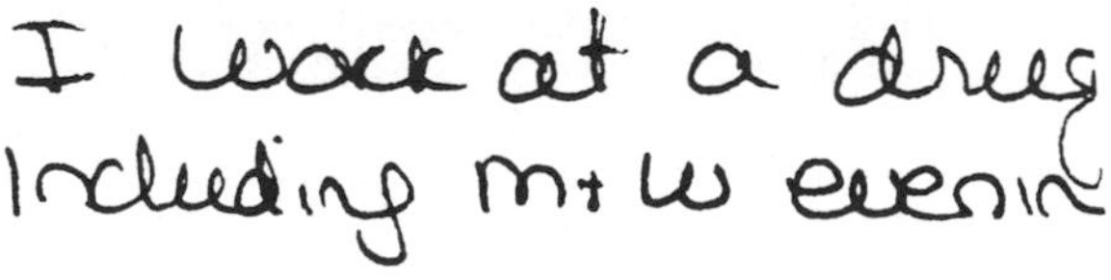

Figure 58.

In Figure 58 we have a young girl with a naive handwriting. She will not talk about her love life. A rather unspontaneous, careful, nice person who is also somewhat formal and conventional.

In addition to arches, Figure 59 has a leanness about it too. Here is a cold person, also shown by the slight backhand slant. The slowness of this sample denotes careful thought in everything she does.

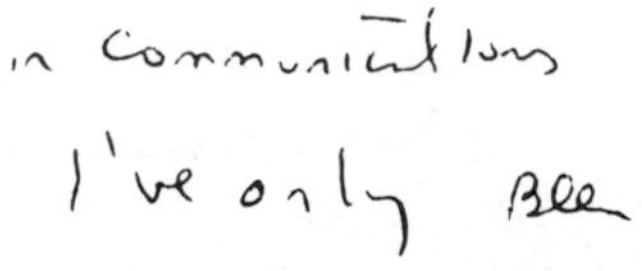

Figure 59.

The arcade shows up again in Figure 60, which exhibits all the characteristics of the person who fears communication. The word endings are abrupt, a sign for aloofness, especially in a straight script. Figure 60 shows a writer who hesitates a great deal, and her slow, ducking, falling shapes belong to the weak, shy person, someone whose life cannot have been a happy one. The arcades underline an uptight woman. The fractured letters point to inner turmoils and difficulties.

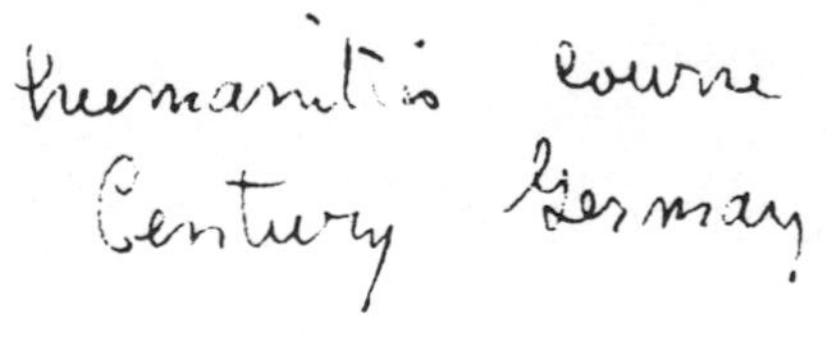

Figure 60.

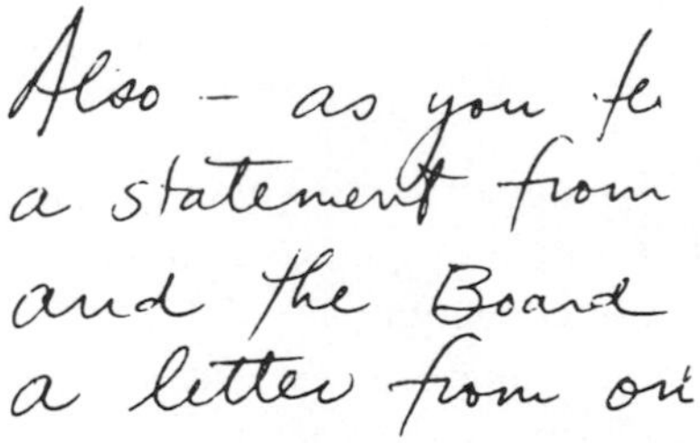

Figure 61.

Finally, by way of contrast, the writing in Figure 61 is easy to like; it has artistry, balance, and grace. Everything about the script is clear; no adornments, no phoniness, no game playing.

To sum up some of the traits and possibilities inherent in the garland and arcade writer see the detailed table below. Note that as always, the sign "+" (plus) refers to a superior handwriting while the "−" (minus) stands for the inferior Formniveau.

GARLAND		ARCADE	
+FN	*−FN*	*+FN*	*−FN*
Plus	**Minus**	**Plus**	**Minus**
Naturalness	Chatty	Keeps secrets	Distrust
Openness	Overly	Sense of	Lack of
Receptiveness	impressionable	etiquette	openness
Frankness	Pushover	Tact	Prudence
Obliging, kind	Withdrawn (in	Thoughtful	Naivete
Adaptability	narrow script)	Aristocratic	Conceals
Able to give in	Easy to influence	Architectural	feelings
Tolerance		and artistic	Repressions
Human			Uptight
			Asocial

One other stroke connection should be mentioned; it is the "thready" link, which makes the writing look almost formless. The thread is the fastest of all links, and the writer, whose mind seems to race ahead, reaches the right margin more rapidly than any other type of writer. The hand can hardly keep up with the pace.

There is a price to pay for thready connections. For one thing, the script often becomes almost illegible, and generally looks snakelike. A person may resort to this flattened-out, hardly legible handwriting, or to such a signature at a special period in his life. Richard Nixon's writing, for instance, deteriorated into a mere strokeless line during the Watergate breakup. The signature was strongly formed fifteen years earlier, and still powerful ten years prior to his resignation. Was it the Watergate trauma that caused the "thread" line? Not so, according to Felix Lehmann, handwriting expert on the Manhattan courts. "A personality intentionally unclear to leave room for maneuvers and deception," Lehmann observed.

There is no doubt that the personality of a thread writer is not what appears on the surface. A person may seem unselfish and open upon first impression, but the contrary could be true. Dr. Pulver called the thready writer "eel-like." To be sure, in a superior script, the thready connector possesses mental dexterity, shrewdness, adaptability, versatility, and finesse. Diplomatic skills are found in a high-caliber thread like that of Dr. Kissinger. (See Figure 62.) Daniel Anthony's delineation of this type: "Diplomatic duplicity . . . intellectual disdain for the rest of us . . ."

HENRY KISSINGER

Figure 62.

If the thread occurs only at the end of each word, the verdict is a positive one. The writer employs a fine wire rather than a jackhammer to get inside another person; that is, the writer has insight. The thinning end stroke is therefore often found among psychiatrists, psychologists, and social workers.

In a quality handwriting—and even the thready connection can be combined with quality—you can deduce other favorable traits like quick comprehension or versatility. When the writing is as unique as Dr. Kissinger's, one can be sure of an original mind, even in conjunction with the sharp, pugnacious arcades, which may cover up diplomatic intrigues (or the wire taps that this government official ordered so often).

The thread connector attempts to adapt and to overcome obstacles; after all, threads take much less time than do arcades or garlands, if the latter are fully executed. How about negative assessments of the threads? Very often, you will find that the line not only crawls or slithers along but also wavers, which makes it a "sinuous" connection. This kind of writing, along with direction changes and almost total illegibility, puts this thread writer into the lowest FN. Result: The sinuous thread writer (especially one who uses no pressure) must be considered wishy-washy, weak, and insecure. If other signs of dishonesty appear in the hand (such as b's open at the bottom), the thread indicates dishonesty. (Chapter 6 will provide guidelines to analysis of dishonesty versus honesty.)

Sinuous thread types who change the slant within words will also be hypocritical and will be apt to quickly change their friendships as well. The abrupt changes indicate that they would be poor friends indeed. If the thread shows up in a trembling or frequently fractured script, the writer may be physically weak; if the thread appears in a script without crossed t-bars or dotted i's, the person is probably sloppy.

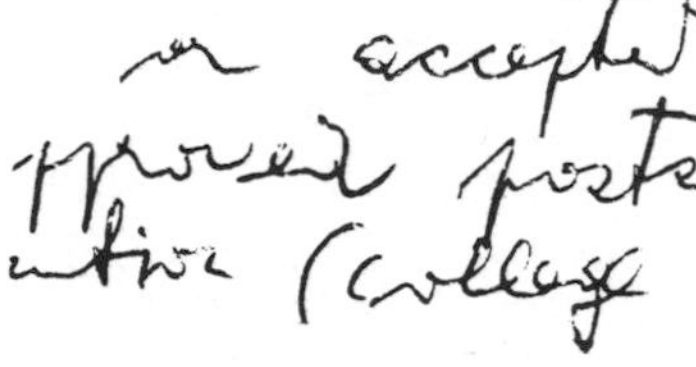

Figure 63.

Figure 63 characterizes the thread of the sinuous writer whose t-bars are crossed, and who exhibits enough pressure to discount the possibility of any weakness. The person is just insecure and somewhat knocked about by life. Totally illegible threads, so Dr. Pulver tells us, always indicate the inconsiderate person.

Disconnections

We can generally assume coherence in a writer who joins all or most of the letters. The thoughts flow freely in such writing samples, as seen in Figures 1, 13, and 46. All these people think logically, and need not pause to reflect on their next move. Simplified upper connections, such as in Figure 39 emphasize mental agility.

Disconnected writing means that there are breaks between most or all of the letters, and, if the FN is high, it can be the telltale sign of a scientist (in small script), poet (affectionate, lean, round formations), person with psychological gifts, or an especially warm individual (end line becomes smaller than balance of the word). Certainly some of the world's greatest poets and philosophers wrote without connections between letters; in a superior hand, the breaks show a bent for meditation and contemplation.

One typical example is that of French philosopher H. Bergson, whose script can be seen in Figure 64. It shows Bergson to be sensitive, thoughtful, and poetic.

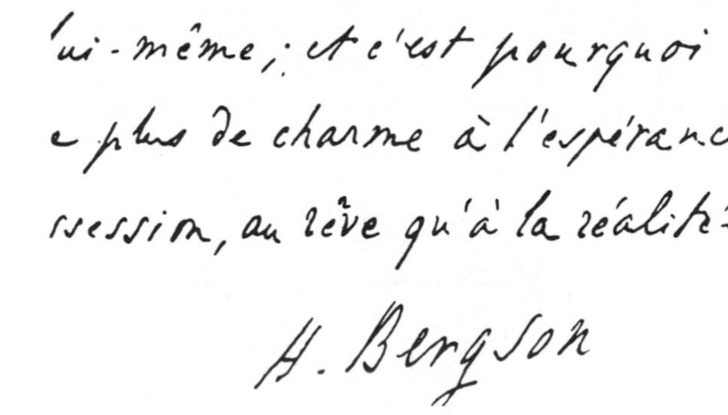

Figure 64.

In a negatively assessed script, the lack of connections tips you off to some sort of disturbance, either in the thought area (upper extensions) or in the phsyical body (many fractures and tremors). If there are also extreme widths between the words, extra wide right margins, and large spaces between the lines, the person dislikes contacts and is basically asocial.

To be sure, none of the above analyses applies to anyone who makes it a point to print every word instead of writing spontaneously. The printer should be encouraged to write more freely for analysis.

As we have already seen, we must attach great significance to disjointed words. If the letters stand apart in a quality handwriting, the person is probably thoughtful, intuitive, capable of contemplation and deep analysis, and an individualist. Scientists and poets often write in a disconnected style. A poor, unrhythmic script with disconnected letters denotes the scatterbrained, the disoriented, or the disorganized. Separate letters thus indicate a lack of cohesion, and an inability to concentrate. The person must pause again and again. In the case of a slow hand, such pauses can show up in the over-cautious, the premeditator. If the breaks are combined with primitive, crude letters, we must conclude that the writer has little experience in penmanship.

How about the totally fractured letter?

Dr. Pulver and his associates always stressed that such fractures were signs of either an emotional or physical weakness or illness, depending on the appearance of the script. Some writers have experienced such shocks and traumas in their lives that they will be unable to write a complete letter, or link some of its components. Their hand is as fatigued as their psyche. It is possible to overcome these limping qualities so that some of the letters and words become whole once more. An interesting example of a fractured, depressed personality appears below (Figure 65). Figure 66, by contrast, displays a high FN in a most thoughtful hand.

up of prospcative

Figure 65.

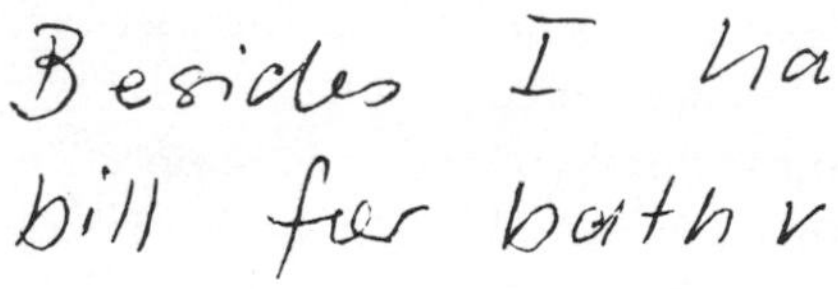

Besides I ha
bill fer bath r

Figure 66.

The following table lists the traits connected with spaces between letters.

CONNECTED LETTERS		DISCONNECTED LETTERS	
+FN	*−FN*	*+FN*	*−FN*
Plus	**Minus**	**Plus**	**Minus**
Logic	Haste	Scientific or poetic inclinations	Disturbances
Thinking speed		Intuition	Asocial trends
Naturalness		Psychological gifts	Loners
		Ability to meditate	Scatterbrained
		Thoughtfulness	

Rigidity Versus Looseness

We have mentioned angular, round, arcaded, garlanded, and thready writing; a detailed analysis can zero in on still other patterns. How rigid does the script appear? Does it seem cramped and hard? Does the execution of strokes stick to one system, without ever departing from it? Does the hand seem to goose-step stiffly? Or is the opposite true, resulting in loose, doughy, pasty writing?

Naturally there is a middle course, which applies to most of the specimens you analyze. You may wish to look back at Figures 47 and 52 for examples of the middle course. The samples are neither harsh, nor doughy, like that in Figure 19, or in the next Figure, 67.

Extreme rigidity occupies the opposite pole. You will find some excellent examples in Figures 5, 43, 49 and 54. Another excellent illustration of rigidity appears below (Figure 68).

Naturally, some handwritings are simply loose, relaxed, and sinuous, without being doughy like that in Figure 67. A typically slack script wavers; it lacks pressure and backbone. Indeed, it can become as formless as in Figure 69, which is hard to decipher.

Figure 67.

Figure 68.

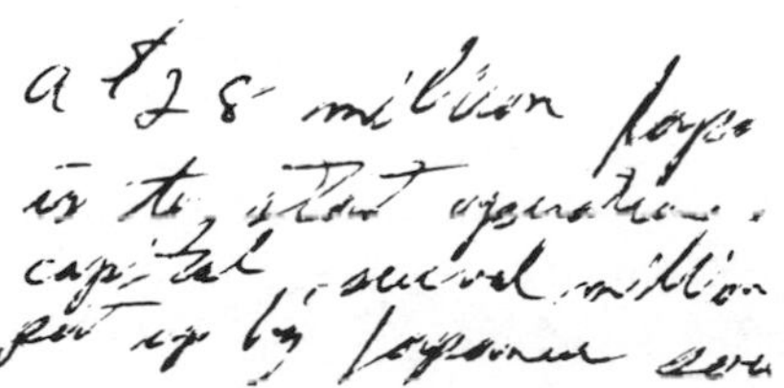

Figure 69.

What is the meaning of rigidity versus looseness or pastiness? The latter is the easiest to explain. Handwriting such as seen in Figure 19 and Figure 67 admirably illustrates the rounded, inky writer's interest in the good life. When you find large lower loops as well, you may be sure of the gourmet, someone keenly interested in good foods, or the sensualist. Such a broad doughy style occurs in both men and women (Figure 67 is a man noted for his knowledge of Scandinavian delicacies). If you see many ink spots in these looped scripts, you can assume that the person has strong erotic drives. The libido is prominent in the oversized lower g extension (Figure 19). The right-hand slant strengthens the assessment of the warm lover. In a larger, rapid script, all these graphological signs point to someone who exhibits a *joie de vivre*, one who truly enjoys life.

Rigid writing suggests something altogether different. The overly hard penmanship of Figure 68, for instance, means stiffness and an ungiving person. The exaggerated pressure belongs to someone who cannot be dissuaded from a viewpoint. Some scripts come with the additional pattern of tightness. All the letters and strokes are close together. Such rigid writers are generally cramped, overly cautious, and self-controlled, even if they maintain a high FN. They are always in control of their impulses, especially if the writing does not lean but is at a backward angle of ninety degrees (meaning the head rules the emotions, of course).

When the rigid script appears orderly, and contains small hooks, the writer is tenacious; if the capitals are sparse and tall, they delineate a sense of etiquette, a formal nature, often found in diplomats. A stiff handwriting always implies that the person is somewhat inhibited. This applies even to the most superb hands, which belong to the most stable individuals.

How about the opposite pole, that of too little rigidity? Figure 69 is typical of this group, as is the sample in Figure 70, characterized by an even more extreme formlessness.

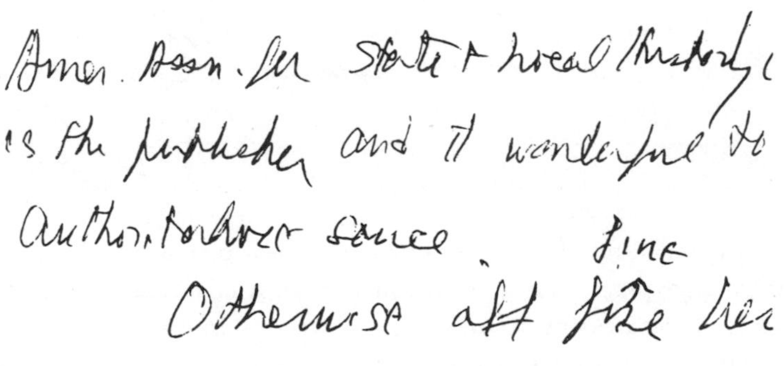

Figure 70.

One might say that this man has been through the wringer, emotionally or physically. The pen can hardly stand the strain of writing. Here is an extreme case of slackness that stems more from temporary exhaustion than from lack of stability or absence of character. The handwriting at this point lacks vigor in all areas. The person is totally fatigued. In a low Formniveau, a lack of rigidity can be interpreted in several ways, depending on other corroborating graphic signs. Here is a detailed list, compiled by my colleague Felix Klein of New York City, showing the possibilities.

LACK OF RIGIDITY

	−FN
	Minus
Letting one's self go	**Lack of discipline**
Weakness	**Disorderliness**
Weak resistance	**Aimlessness**
Changeableness	**Absentmindedness**
Inconstancy	**Restlessness**
Spinelessness	**Uncertainty**
Laxity	**Irritability**
Difficulties in maintaining effort	**Touchiness**
Lack of restraint	**Leaving one's self open to diverting influences**

Some of these traits will show up along with other graphological signs in this book; in the meantime, however, it might be pointed out that one should be cautious in making negative interpretations based on a single letter or word formation. Handwriting analysis always demands the examination of the whole picture together with specific signs. Thus a negative sign may be wiped out by overriding positive signs.

Can formless (loose) writing also indicate positive traits? The answer is yes. If the FN is extremely high, as in the relaxed sample in Figure 71, the looseness can be interpreted as adaptability. One might also point to extremely round writers, many of whom have appeared on preceding pages, whose lack of rigidity often identifies the pleasant, compliant, affable and friendly person.

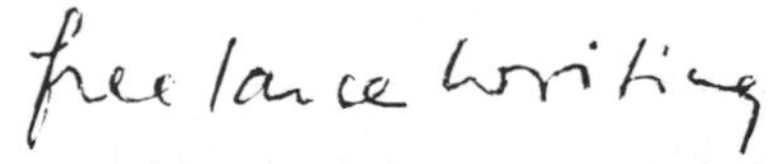

Figure 71.

Pen Pressure

Some writers exert great force on the pen as they race across the paper. This can be a sign of vitality and drive. If you turn over the original copy of the paper, you can actually see and feel the ridges on the back of the page. Indeed, some writers actually break through the paper with their pens. Such heavy pressure can be produced by a delicate person as easily as by one with great physical strength. It often means that the writer feels strongly about something, that he or she is intense and has willpower.

Light pressure, on the other hand, can belong to the writer who takes life less seriously and forgets unpleasant incidents quickly. Such a gentle writer forgives easily. Light-pressured writing generally goes along with sensitivity and refinement. These writers avoid battles. They prefer the smooth path instead, and you will often find that, apart from the light pressure, there are other indicators, such as round script.

All of the above is not to say that a light imprint on paper necessarily has to do with a lack of emotion; the contrary may be true if there is an extreme right-hand lean as well. The light-pressure people can be passionate, even if their pens float across the paper.

Dr. Pulver points out that some persons "aim to surmount all obstacles, to remove all irritations" by skimming lightly across the page. To be sure, if the absence of pressure (along with a lack of rigidity) occurs in a formless script, the writer may be sickly, or at the mercy of all influences. Avoiding crossing t-bars, fractured letters, changing direction—accompanied by lack of pressure—can all be indicators of the weak-willed individual, or at least one who lacks energy. In addition, Felix Klein discovered that there may be a lack of depth.

The power writer is altogether different, as we have seen. The script of the hotel manager in Figure 5 and the German woman in Figure 56 both combine pressure with a good FN. They are both strong people, with a fine vitality, decisiveness, and poise. Strong pressure in superior hands can also indicate poise, initiative, determination, and the capacity to "live it up" on many fronts. A most intriguing picture emerges in the next sample (Figure 72) because here pressure is combined with rigidity. The FN is excellent. There is good balance, rhythm and geometry. Here is the disciplined individual who gets things done.

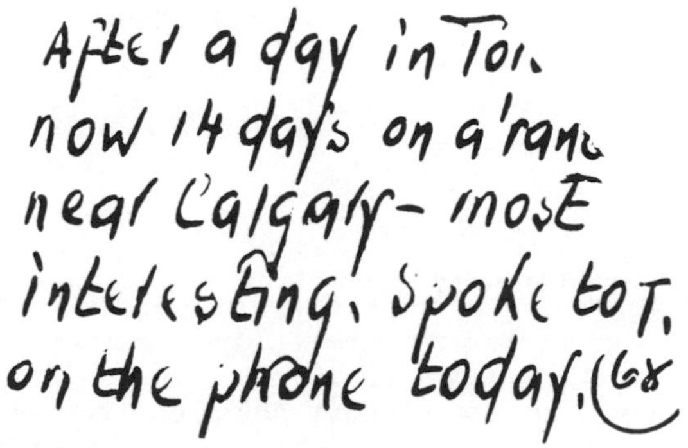

Figure 72.

What if the pressure increases so much that the pen pierces the paper? Arabic calligraphy can do this. Most of the strokes are piercing. After all, some Arab tribes still chop off the hands of thieves and tear out the tongues of traitors. The "cutting edge" of Arabic calligraphy reminds one of a piercing method of killing.

Certain Russian scripts, notably that of Stalin, have the earmarks of such ruthlessness and brutality. Even the "civilized" modern American businessman can exhibit a trend toward ruthless tactics. A typical sample was shown in Figure 18. An inferior script, along with much pressure, such as is seen in Figure 51 (which is also worth studying for its lack of rhythm), belongs to the contrary, argumentative, unpleasant person.

The opposite applies to the pleasant writer in Figure 29, or to the highly sensitive French philosopher Bergson (Figure 64) who used no pressure whatsoever. The following table sums up the important points covered.

MUCH PEN PRESSURE		**LITTLE PRESSURE**	
+FN	*−FN*	*+FN*	*−FN*
Plus	**Minus**	**Plus**	**Minus**
Intensity	Harshness	Sensitivity	Lack of energy
Vitality	Ruthlessness	Adaptability	Lack of poise
Initiative	Brutality	Humility	Sickly
Decisiveness	Lack of consideration	Refinement	Lack of resistance
Living to the hilt	Aggressiveness	Lack of depth	
Getting things done	Defiance		
Determination	Bluntness (jackhammer types)		
Poise	Obstinacy		

How about writers who use medium pressure? They obviously compromise. Their feelings and sensitivities are well-balanced. They are well adjusted on various levels.

Heavy Writing

Strong pressure is often confused with heavy writing. You recognize the latter by its slowness. The pressure appears willed and artificial. Some writings exhibit heaviness only in the capitals, with the rest of the word gliding across the paper. In other writings the pen digs in only at the end of each word.

Some explanations are therefore in order about the phenomenon of heavy penmanship. Few graphologists mention this possibility. However, one of those who does is Dr. Max Pulver, who emphasizes that such heaviness always destroys the rhythm. He considers that writers with artificial pressure suffer from a heaviness of spirit. They may carry too great a personal burden, or they may have a melancholy nature.

The interpretation is interesting, and applies to Figure 73. The writer is a widow who had suffered many of life's blows. Additionally, the bent "t's" and "f's" show this. One can easily spot the impact of bad news. Figure 68 also shows the painstaking slowness of a heavy-hearted person who has become rigid and unbending under life's blows.

has been fascinating
and most informat

Figure 73.

What if only the beginnings are thickened? According to Dr. Pulver, this denotes a person who wants to appear important, who aims for effects, or who wants to pretend some nonexistent clout and poise in business. Pulver ascribed such accentuated capitals to minor clerks or lower-echelon businessmen as well as to the *nouveau riche*. If the pressure in the capitals is accompanied by major adornments, the person wants to show off and will have a tendency to brag. A characteristic script appears in Figure 74.

Figure 74.

There is still one other graphic possibility—the pressure appears only at the end of each word. In this case, you can assume a nature who likes to bark orders. (The dictatorial tendency can be backed by strong, umbrella-type t-bar crossings.) Pulver also discovered that some writers who use pressure at the end are garrulous and quarrelsome—they always want to be right.

4

Space and Motion

You will also encounter handwritings where the pause only occurs intermittently. For instance, there is no connection after the i. The reason is that the writer stops for an instant to place an i-dot, a matter which he or she considers important. (In a neat handwriting, such pauses show reliability and conscientiousness.) Intermittent breaks may also show up toward the end of a page as the writer's muscles begin to tire.

Space between Capitals and Letters

One of the most interesting occurrences of disjointed letters, however, is apt to occur at the beginning of a word, especially when the word is capitalized. Analysis of the white space that follows a capital is of prime importance in judging human beings. The capital *always* represents the ego. It gives us an insight into how one feels about oneself. The balance of the word—any word—is the other person; that is, family, friends, society, and the world.

According to Dr. Pulver, the lone first letter or capital (which from now on will be referred to as "caps") in an otherwise connected word belongs to the person who stands apart from others. How far apart? That depends on the distance and the overall size of the script, on the frequencies of the pauses, and on the shapes of the caps themselves. An excellent example of a capital formation can be seen in Figure 75.

The caps are not only separate but also rolled into themselves. The "C" in "Curtis" is particularly revealing in that respect. What do such shell-like motions indicate? The inward roll simply means selfishness, in addition

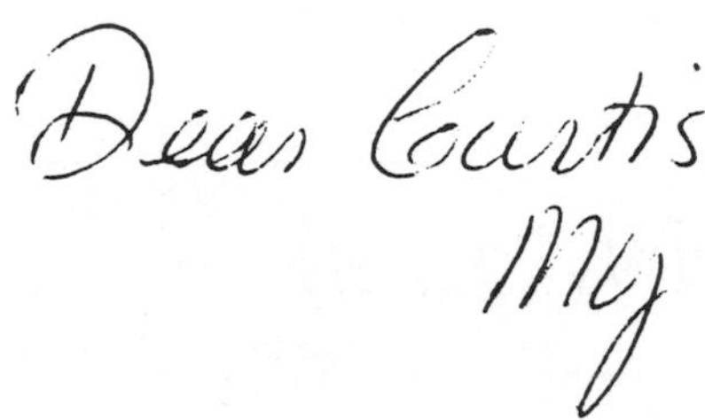

Figure 75.

to "apartness." In short, the person stands alone because the ego comes first. When egocentricity is also underlined by strong pen pressure in a writing such as that in Figure 75, we can be sure of an individual who must always have his or her way with others.

The disconnected first letter or capital can also crop up in a sensitive, gentle, pressureless script like that in Figure 76. The separation between the capital and the balance of each word denotes shyness, fear and delicacy. The letters stand fearfully, timidly apart here, and the writing shows no pressure (or strength) at all. The letters themselves are narrow, revealing anxiety. Indeed, the writing is so thin and frail that it can be bent in the wind, like a dry weed on a mountain slope.

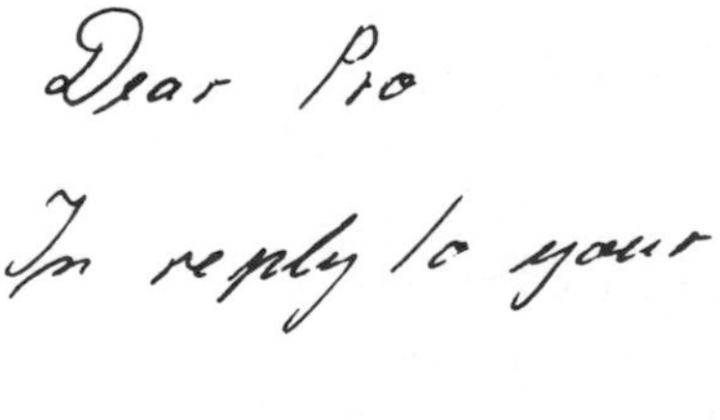

Dear Pro
In reply to your

Figure 76.

We have also seen such sensitive hands combined with good rhythm and good balance, as in Figure 61. (Note the excellent connections of the caps with other letters.) Another characteristically positive illustration contrasts all the more with the two preceding ones. The daring, socially fluent handwriting is of a former social worker who married the governor of a western state. One glance at the "C's" in Figure 77 is enough to spot a congenial, courageous, and friendly woman who does not fear, but welcomes rapport with others.

Figure 77.

Space between Words

It was not until Dr. Max Pulver's life-long graphological studies in Switzerland that we knew much about the meanings of white space between words. We know now that these spaces are related to the writer's need to reach out (or not reach out) to others. The distances between words give you an idea about the writer's attitude toward other human beings and the need for contact and involvement.

The writers of Figures 8 and 64, although of different nationalities, both cared for other humans. (Note how close the words appear on paper.) By contrast, the writer in Figure 77 kept her distance between the first, middle initial, and last name.

In the best writing, much space between words points to someone who is profound, contemplative, and perhaps prudent. Certainly the well-controlled writer who pauses *thinks* before acting. If the pauses become extreme, perhaps longer than the words themselves, we are clearly face-to-face with an aloof person. Such distances are easy enough to detect. The opposite condition, that is, the absence of separating space, can also be obvious. Its meaning makes sense. The person who almost joins each terminal stroke to the first letter of the following word generally likes people and seeks contacts with others.

The pausing writers prize their own distance from others and their objectivity. Many truly aristocratic persons write in this manner. In an overly rigid script, however, extreme spacing generally shows isolation or even alienation. Each word is an island, showing that the writer treasures his or her private spaces to such an extent that isolation can result. These feelings and needs can also show up in the disconnected capitals.

A pronounced case of isolation—a woman who refuses to date and has few friends—can be witnessed in Figure 78 below. (As you will see later, her right margins are extremely large, indicating further distance from her peers.)

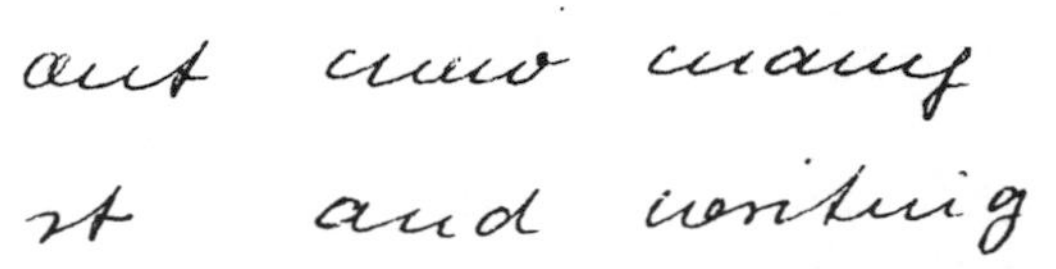

Figure 78.

How about *uneven* spacing between words? Such a situation is common among youth, but it can also be found in older people who are not sure about what they want. They may relate well to one person and poorly to another.

Right Margins

When it comes to our relationships with others, certain margins on a large sheet of paper are most revealing, particularly the right margin. The rest of the world, others, society, are represented by the right margins, just as the second and remaining letters of each word symbolize other human beings (a discovery made by Dr. Pulver).

Schools or parents tell us little about how far to go toward the right edge of a letterhead. The right margin is therefore up to the writer who can lift the pen and start a new line, according to personal wishes. The margin thus reflects certain deep-down attitudes to the world.

Just as the distances between words are meaningful, so is the distance from the last word to the right edge of the paper. The space can be enormous; a few people actually stop in the middle or two-thirds of the way. Such excessive white space doubtlessly denotes someone who aims to preserve his or her distance from others. When a large right-hand margin also appears in a left-tipped script, the person is reserved indeed. Many loners favor such exaggerated right-hand margins, as do the shy and fearful.

It is also intriguing to encounter scripts that somehow crash and splinter as they bang against the right margin. The latter may approach as quickly and as unexpectedly as the rapids to the imprudent canoeist. Result? The canoe collides with a rock and the last word comes apart against the paper's edge, its pieces hanging either up or down. Youthful students often move so impulsively across the paper, as do the thoughtless, the unprepared and the unorganized.

Left Margins

The left margins are equally interesting in another sense. Etiquette books tell us that it is proper to reserve some white space to the left. There are writers who do not, of course. One might call them the rebels who do what they want to do.

In some cases, the resulting widening margins are unconscious. If the writer becomes more enthusiastic, the left margin will grow wider as eagerness increases. Such a habit points to someone who gets involved in a task or a relationship. It is a good sign, for the widening left margin moves toward the *right*, and therefore toward other people.

Graphologists universally make some other deductions as well. Is the left margin very wide or extremely narrow, for instance? Does the writer use up or conserve space? Surely, the extremely narrow (or even non-existent) margin must belong to the thrifty person. If we economize on paper we are likely to economize in other areas as well, especially financial ones. In brief, you will seldom be wrong if you interpret an overly narrow left margin, along with full upper and lower spaces, as the sign of a frugal person; for example, the homemaker who uses up leftovers, or the businessman who makes the most of his employees' time. Such narrow margins can occur in harmonious, pleasant scripts such as seen in Figure 79, that of a devoted nurse. Her training at home led to her great sense of thrift and opposition to wastefulness.

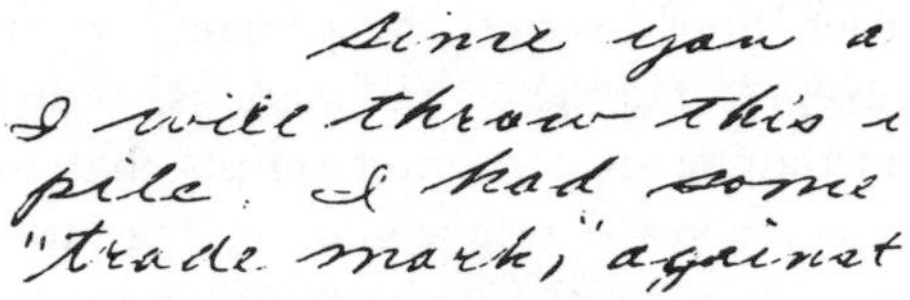

Since you a
I will throw this i
pile. I had some
"trade mark," against

Figure 79.

Upper Margins

What if there is little or no upper margin? Two possibilities emerge. Either the writer is supremely extroverted and eager to be in touch with others or, in the case of a low FN, the individual is intrusive and overbearing; a clinging vine. More clues can be found in exaggerated left or right slants, too much pen pressure, overblown capitals (indicating conceit), or strokes that roll inward to the left (selfishness). If the upper margin is extreme, the writer wants to keep his or her distance from the addressee, or even from the rest of humanity.

The Lower Margin

When only the bottom margin is wide, the situation resembles that of the exaggerated right-hand margin. In both instances there is restraint or inhibition. Such writers often fear others, or, if they exhibit mainly positive graphic signs, they need an inordinate amount of privacy (artists and scholars). The reverse is often found, too. At the bottom there is only a tiny wedge of space, or the writer fills the sheet to the edge. This may be interpreted similarly to the narrow left margins. The individual uses all the available space. It is generally a sign of careful spending, of a Yankee's desire to save space and make do. In a very cramped, narrow script, there is a tendency to miserliness.

Margins: Final Observations

There remains one other possibility. Some writers manage to convey a marvellous sense of balance, indeed, beauty, by means of margins. Their writing sits artistically in the provided space, with left, right, top and bottom margins in balance. Such people usually have a fine sense of aesthetics. They are the architects, photographers, artists, designers and printers. The picture of their page includes how they handle lines; never so close together that their writing is illegible, nor so far apart as to waste space. A final reminder—margins can only be judged on full paper, and not on scraps or postcards.

MARGINS

	+FN **Plus**	*−FN* **Minus**
Left Margin		
Wide	Good taste, good manners, generosity, sense of luxury	Snobbishness, pretense
Widening	Enthusiasm, eager for involvement, caught up by action	Impulsiveness, impatience, losing battle against self-control
Narrow	Thrift	Miserliness
Narrowing	Increasing caution, seeing through others	Withdrawing, inability to give
Right Margin		
Wide	Sense of etiquette, sense of privacy	Alienation, isolation
Widening		Gradual withdrawal
Narrow	Attempts to be social, likes people	Uninhibited, lacks organization

Line Arrangement in Space

The study of line separation is another important factor in space analysis.

A well organized individual, whether an executive or an artist, will generally strive for legibility and intelligent use of space. This always means clear demarcations; that is, no tangled lines. For that reason, overlapping graphic elements always lower the Formniveau, a fact worth remembering. For a fresh look at some high FN's, see Figures 24, 45, 52, and 64.

Lines that are so closely packed together that they cannot be read show a writer who cannot keep his or her ideas properly organized. Figures 7 and 23 show two samples of this. Such writing is a sign of a disorderly and confused mind. Lack of space between lines also indicates a lack of intelligence. In the case of an otherwise original, well-formed script, scissor-like formations and lower loops cutting into the upper extensions in the line below always belong to a ruthless person. Such ruthlessness is further corroborated by the use of strong pressure. There are many such examples in this book. (See if you can find some.)

It is true that, while some people pack their lines too tightly, others put only a few words on a page. Extreme distances again mean that the person lacks contact with others for a variety of reasons, which can range from timidity to an overblown self-esteem to a creative person's need for private spaces.

Dr. Pulver has collected examples where only a few words appear in one line (or on the entire page). He calls such writers inconsiderate. They obviously "consume too much."

Baseline Direction

How do the lines themselves look? Do they waver as the pen travels across the page? Or are they consistently straight? (Here is one reason why we recommend unlined paper. Lined paper offers too much of a crutch to the writer.) It is obvious that the shortest distance between two points is a straight line. In graphology it means that the shortest distance to a writer's goal is the straight unwavering baseline. People who can stick to one direction show good control of their pens and of life. An arrow-like baseline therefore belongs to the goal-conscious, indicating an absence of (or at least a control of) moods. By contrast, some writers show a disturbing up and down trend in their lives. They are easily influenced by adverse trends or are bowled over by obstacles, a situation that is further documented by constant slant changes as well. Such topsy-turvy writing denotes the temperamental, the illogical and the disturbed. An outstanding example is seen in Figure 80.

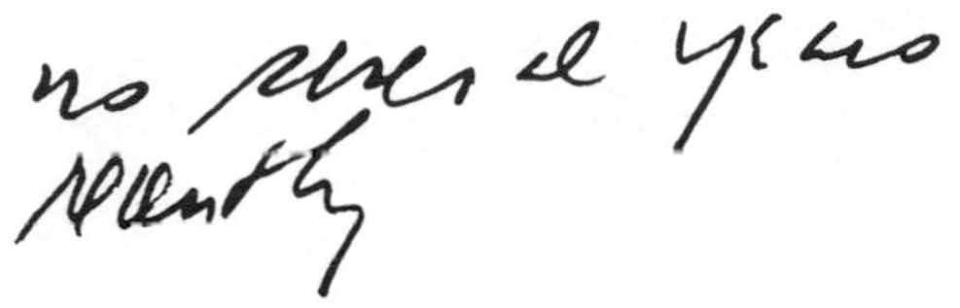

Figure 80.

Apart from the completely erratic baseline, the writing is totally loose, without backbone or substance, the sign of a weak character structure, a person who is easily influenced, untrustworthy.

In the young, erratic changes of direction are normal. A teenager is at the mercy of many moods and can hardly be expected to write a straight baseline. The age of your correspondent is important when you judge alignment. An eighty-year-old man, for example, is apt to lose control over the muscles of his hand and fingers, so that wavering lines can be normal.

Ascending Lines

When you consider the direction of the baseline you must also consider whether it slants upward or downward or remains horizontal. If the writing consistently moves upward it usually signals the optimist, the person with faith in the future. The dynamic doers of the world often couple their somewhat large scripts with an uphill trend. The sample in Figure 81 for instance, was written by an optimistic, positive, active executive.

Such climbing lines often convey not only optimism but also ambition. It is wise to check several samples over a period of weeks or months. Does the writing always climb sharply or only on the occasion of the current analysis? In the latter case, the optimistic mood may be temporary.

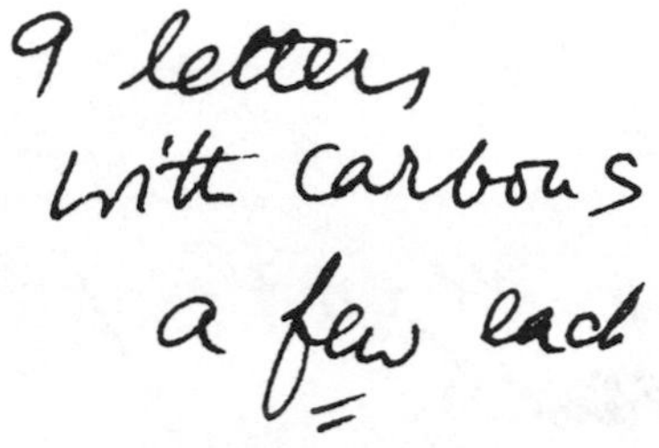

Figure 81.

Figure 82.

The Falling Baseline

Even the earliest graphologists were in agreement about falling lines, interpeting them as signs of depression and pessimism. Modern analysts, Dr. Pulver among them, added that the sinking line should be interpreted as exhaustion. It could be physical (the writer has no strength left to maintain horizontal direction) or purely emotional exhaustion, such as the trauma of divorce or the death of someone close, for instance. The skilled graphologist looks for other indicators. These include fractured letters, lack of pressure, sudden downward collapsing letters or bent t's or l's, such as we encountered in Figure 73. Incompleted strokes, ducking capitals, and other aberrations, which we saw in Figure 70, along with sudden direction changes of the falling line add to the exhaustion syndrome.

The sinking trend, without all of the above additional problems (such as in Figure 82), generally belongs to a depressed person. In this case the writing is of a chronically depressed woman who feels hopeless about the world around her. (Please note the direction of Figures 81 and 82.)

A word of caution seems in order, however. All humans are occasionally at the mercy of strains or moods and most become depresed at some point in their lives. If at the time of writing one is in a down mood it will be reflected in falling lines. The writing returns to normal when the situation has improved. It is for this reason we suggest you obtain not just one but several writing samples. They should come from differing periods in a person's life.

Other Line Patterns

If a baseline can climb or fall steadily it can also form a stair-like pattern, which shows that the writer attempts to battle the fall. The battle may be lost in the end because the line plunges anyway, but the staircase pattern points to the valiant fight. If a baseline descends gradually, reaching its deepest down curve in the middle of the page, the person began with a measure of pessimism but eventually overcame it by rising toward the right margin. The situation may also be the opposite. After a brief ascent that peaks in the middle of the page, the writer's pen sinks once more. Here an individual shows some spunk, but unfortunately gives up in the end.

Envelopes

One might presume that a person pays special attention to addressing an envelope, that for once legibility becomes paramount and thus yields no information about character. This is not so, however.

Many writers cannot hide their true nature when penning an address. Others put up a front. Their script may vary from that inside the letter itself. An individual may write in a moderately affectionate slant in the letter itself; outside, on the envelope (or postcard), the same person unexpectedly assumes a 90-degree angle.

What are the reasons? Actually, the writer wants to appear or remain cool toward the addressee. In some cases, such as hand-addressed business letters, there seems no need for warmth, hence the straight script on an envelope.

By the same token, the aesthetically pleasing use of space on a stamped envelope often emerges as well. The name, street address, and city can be as handsomely arranged as an artist's drawing. Or, conversely, all may seem lopsided, telling us that the writer possesses little sense of beauty.

The inner person emerges as well. Elation or depression will be shown by ascending or falling lines. The condition could be temporary or, if it shows up on every envelope, it could be chronic. Dr. Pulver also attaches great symbolic importance to an address tucked away in the bottom left or right-hand corner of an envelope. According to the Swiss researcher, it means that the writer "crawls into a corner" out of shyness or fear.

Figures

Dr. Pulver further reminds us to watch for the execution of figures. If they are oversized, along with oversized businesslike lower loops, the person cares a great deal about money. If the figures are small, they should at least be sharp and clear. Sloppy undersized numerals generally indicate people who have little fiscal interest and who perhaps cannot manage money.

Past and Future

When we speak of lines, space, and movement, we must also point out an important graphological discovery of the twentieth century. In moving across the paper from left to right, the pen wants to communicate with other people. The right therefore symbolizes the rest of the world as well as the future. It follows then that the left is the self and the past.

These are important considerations in analyzing capitals and the balance of words, right margins, shell-like letter forms, and strokes directed toward the left. In a poetic, artistic hand, such left movements, expressed in d's or in terminal strokes, point to a preoccupation with the past, common in older people. If the (warm) slant bears out this tendency, you will have before you a rather sentimental or nostalgic person. Terminal strokes that lead consistently to the right (some typical ones appeared in Figure 24) show outgoing personal ties. Left-hand movement in a low FN, such as in Figures 65 and 83, spells selfishness (note terminal stroke) or narcissistic tendencies.

To be sure, exceptions also exist for the hand that heads toward the right. There is, for instance, the drift to the right with a brutal, club-like end

Figure 83.

Figure 84.

Figure 85.

pressure. If the script is also angular, the pressure-heavy terminal stroke indicates that the writer actually rejects other people, under the guise of being outgoing. Endings may harpoon downward into the material zone. Here is the concealed search for personal financial advantage. (See Figure 150.) Terminal strokes can also reach out to the right, only to hook upward and backward, such as the "you" in Figure 85 (note the cold backward slant). Here is another sign of acquisitiveness, or, as in this case, rapaciousness.

If the script itself is extremely tight (a situation discussed in previous chapters) the long finale does not change the basic uptightness or lack or generosity. If the writing swings back left through the name or in fact through any word, self-deprecating or self-destructive impulses can be suspected

5

Capitals and Individual Letters

We have waited until now to touch on capitals and individual letters. Why wait so long? It is because graphologists insist upon considering a script *as a whole first*, and only toward the end of their analysis do they focus on individual letters of the alphabet. This is not so for the graphoanalysts, whose system leans to a great extent on crossed t-bars and dotted i's. (Graphoanalysts learn these principles in a few easy lessons. No genuine interest in people or background in psychology is required.)

Capital Letters

It should be stated from the outset that one must not underestimate the importance of individual letters, particularly the capitals, which stand out. Capitals represent the writer in more ways than one, and yield many insights. They overshadow the rest of the letters and by standing out become advertisements for the individual's characteristics.

Much of what we have learned about slant, zones, size and width is further borne out in the caps. Here we see the most revealing proof of a person's ego. A cap's size tells all about how we see ourselves. You need only to study the grandiose, overblown signature of, for example, Jacqueline Kennedy Onassis (Figure 123), or of certain film stars, to realize the extent of their egos. Their caps can be five, even seven, times as high as the rest of the word.

Outsized capitals always point to grossly exaggerated egos. A good example was seen in Figure 34 ("John"). Its enormous size (complete with angles) signalled arrogance. Other very large caps express pride (if a high FN is present) and conceit (adornments). We do not need to examine the individual letters to emphasize now that slightly higher than average caps in a good script spell quality. The caps in Figure 61, for instance, show professional pride and striving for practicality (note simplification of "B"). The tall "C's" in the sample of the governor's wife (Figure 77) denote class. This woman is aware of who she is and has no pretensions. (Compare the pretentious person who furnished the sample in Figure 75.)

If you combine too much size with too much sideward expansion, as in the next sample, Figure 86, you get a capital that shouts vanity and hungers for notoriety; a show-off.

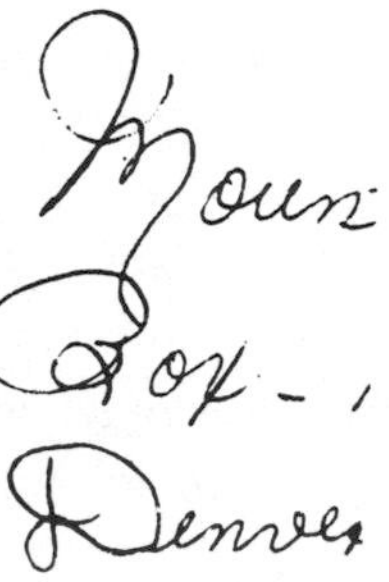

Figure 86.

Except for Figure 77, the above-mentioned caps all lack true elegance. The letter formations appear awkward, unncessarily adorned with arabesques. The "M" and the "B" of Figure 86 are all too common (for example, clumsily over dressed women who favor hats of plastic fruit). You will find many such writings in this book, and all around you as well.

Capitals always tell us something about someone's self-concept. The woman of Figure 86 thinks of herself as elegantly dressed. She has decided that more is better, but succeeds only in making a negative impression. Such fussy, ostentatious, and garish writing tells you that the writer desires admiration and respect, but has little basis for it. In contrast, the writer of Figure 61, another woman, has a healthy self-concept, is secure in her achievements, and accepts recognition for her accomplishments. Slightly adorned capitals often merely indicate an old-fashioned Victorian sense.

Dear Bunny:
It was so thoughtful of
to send us the issue of W
That had all those fascinat

Figure 87.

It is always intriguing to observe someone's departure from the copybook pattern once taught at school. The caps especially lend themselves to drastic innovations. A writer may complicate her B's and other caps, or simplify them, as we have seen in many samples throughout the book (some good ones are Figures 8, 52, and 64). The simplification can be highly original, such as the sample in Figure 87 where the letters "T" and "D" show up a particularly stylish simplification. At the same time, true character comes out in the aforementioned writer of Figure 86 who added all sorts of unnecessary touches to what she learned at school. The individual change of caps can also stem from the rebelliousness of someone who, on purpose, writes illegibly. Only the most compelling inner drive can make someone increase the size of a J five times, when the school model dictates a maximum of 1½ times the middle zone's height.

The reasons for large capitals are summed up below.

LARGE CAPITALS

+FN **Plus**	*−FN* **Minus**
Search for greatness	Arrogance
Poise	Conceit
Pride	Egocentricity
Solid ego	Vanity
Self-confidence	Self-importance

How about small capitals? We have seen these in several positive instances (Figures 8 and 52) as modesty. The person knows (and does not overestimate) his or her place in life—a commendable attitude. Some of the world's greatest figures—Einstein, Churchill, Eisenhower—used fairly small caps.

The modesty of the most likeable individuals can also become so extreme that humility turns into lack of faith in oneself.

The Capital I

The I expresses, more than any other capital, the ego. The I can be as tiny as that in the (already small) Figure 79. Here it stands for extreme humility, taught to this woman by an autocratic father. There are I's that appear still smaller, sometimes barely reaching to the top of the middle zone.

In a handwriting that appears weak, with fractured, shifting direction, the miniature capital I usually denotes feelings of inferiority. Some people even avoid the upper case I, thus expressing their own unworthiness. (We have already discussed the egotistic writer of an inflated, exaggerated capital I, whose smugness can be an irritant to others.)

There are a few other I formations that deserve a hearing. One is the cultured, oversimplified "I" in Figure 52, who made a name for himself as a poet. Another is the frightened, hypersensitive "I" in Figure 76. There are some I's that reflect squashed egos. (See Figure 56.) Finally there is the solidly supported, well-balanced Roman capital in Figure 20. It belongs to a practical, intelligent woman who showed much strength when faced with adversity. The strongly standing (yet not overbearing) "I" shows why she came out on top.

The capital I has a special meaning to the writer. Subconsciously, this letter reveals how the person actually feels about his or her environment.

Other Caps

Almost everything we have discussed applies to other capitals, too. The slowly left-angled capital "M" in Figure 48, for instance, reinforces the first impact of premeditation and falseness. The artistic efforts of the "M" in Figure 86 fail; the letter merely looks awkward and overblown. A capital M that is open usually denotes frankness (the arcade in a captial does not deserve a negative vote, because of a need for legibility). However, it is always interesting to find an arcade M that avoids the rest of the word (and the world), as in Figure 75, or to see an M with the final hump the largest. It is always the hump of the tactless.

There are some letters like the P, for instance, that offer an opportunity for fullness. Since the sail-like form appears in the upper zone, it generally indicates imagination. (A typical such upper loop appears in Figure 10.) Extremely slim caps usually belong to very dry unimaginative people. Perhaps one of the most typical ones appears below, in Figure 88. The capital "G" is compressed, along with the rest of the writing. The "A" is so narrow that it looks like a small dried stalk. The fifty-year-old writer, a spinster, has no imagination whatsoever, which contributes to her life-long situation alone. (Another handicap is her fear of revealing herself to others, to open up. Note the small "m's" and "n's," which are cautiously arcaded.)

Figure 88.

By way of contrast, study Figure 89. The "P" in "Pam" characterizes the imaginative person who also possesses tact and finesse and has an extroverted personality. It is easy to understand why this young woman quickly reached the top of the public relations profession. In her work she represents the town of Vail, Colorado, a resort area that always shows imagination in its publicity.

Figure 89.

Such idea production, which shows up in the P's, J's, and other capital letters, proves useful in business, the arts, theatre and other professions.

Few caps afford the chance to bring the large loop into the lower zone. The J provided that opportunity to the next writer whose balloon-like formations point to imagination as well as sexual interest. This will be touched upon in our discussions of small letters (see below) and of sexuality (in Chapter 6). A good example, Figure 90, serves both occasions. The large

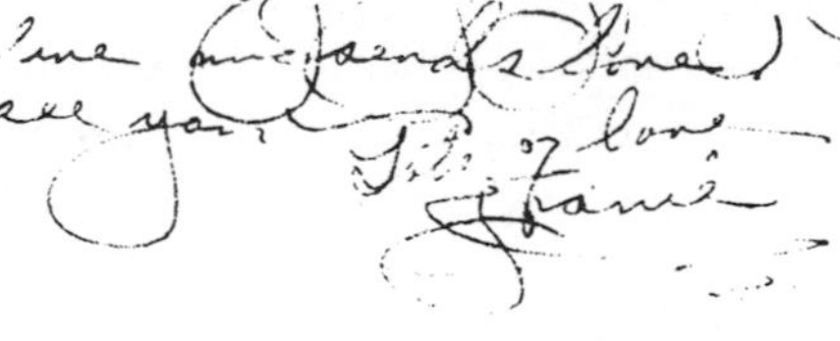

Figure 90.

loop in the signature speaks for itself. Such a full shape in the lower area always has to do with sexual interest.

Simplification of Caps

When speaking of full capitals or adorned capitals, one must also touch upon the simplified capital letter, which we have observed many times throughout this text. There are a number of good reasons for a writer to seek the shortest route. The capital "T's" in the elegant sample in Figure 87 illustrate this shortcut, as does the simple "T" in Figure 8. The reason for such simplifications (which include the "I" in Figure 52) can be the search for the essential, or for practicality. Some writers introduce certain Greek letters in their simplified capitals, which must be interpreted as a bent toward culture. (You will find numerous examples throughout the book.)

In any event, simple letters have generally greater FN value than adorned ones. That is why some of the world's great thinkers often write with an almost deceptive simplicity. These people are down to basics. They have no need to impress anyone else with flourishes and adornments.

The matter of embellishment can be summed up in the accompanying table.

SIMPLIFICATION		EXTREME EMBELLISHMENT	
+FN	*−FN*	*+FN*	*−FN*
Plus	**Minus**	**Plus**	**Minus**
Clear thinking Objectivity Grasping of essentials Style Practicality	Over-simplification Bluntness	Inability to see the woods for the trees Subjectivity By-passing of essentials Complex thinking	Interest in outer appearances only Observance of conventional formalities Awkwardness Clumsiness Artificiality

Small letters

We now come to the part for which graphoanalysis is so well known, namely crossing t-bars, dotting i's, and the meaning of other small letters. Before getting into details as we examine some prominent members of the alphabet, we must mention some general items. First, always interpret more than just an individual letter (for instance, the t). Look also at speed, pressure, size, roundness, angularity, and so on. Second, try to make sure that your discovery (say, a weakly crossed t-bar) occurs frequently enough to count. Look through a large batch of writing to observe several examples of how the t-bar is crossed.

Upper Loops

While we spoke briefly about the lower loops and their sexual or material connotations, the upper loops have to do with man's interest in the intangible, such as religion, philosophy, the human spirit, the occult, and the intellect. The width of the upper loops indicates the degree of our involvement in these spheres.

The above statement affects the loops (or simple strokes) of upper-loop letters such as the l, k, f, h, b, and one of the most graphic, the d. If any of these letters greatly exceed the copybook sample, the person's pursuits are either intellectual (also indicated by Greek or Roman letters), of the occult (large upper loops), or religious (terminal strokes toward the heavens). If the upper sphere is totally neglected, none of these intangibles interest the writer, who often makes up for the gap by exaggerating the lower material zone. On the other hand, a low-grade writing with greatly exaggerated upper loops shows that the writer has too much imagination and lives in a world of fantasy or exaggeration. Some of the best scripts (Figures 64, 77, and 87) strike a good balance.

The Small d

Of all the possibilities, the small d is the most meaningful because it reveals someone's sensitivity, artistry or cultural aspirations.

Some fine composers, for instance, form their d's like notes (or employ musical signs for the f's). Religious authors and other idealists let their d's trail upward into the heavens. However, easily offended artistic natures betray their hypensensitivity with d's that come with a broken head (see Figure 63). A d that arcs considerably to the left speaks of a preoccupation with the past.

Much like other upper (or lower) loop letters, the d need not swing to the right but may head downward instead. The sudden end of a d, or other upper-loop letters like the l and the k, can signify only one thing; a person who does not reach out. Such a cramped attitude, which was evident in the terminal strokes of Figures 22 and 54, among others, can be motivated by inhibitions, fear and distrust of others, unnecessary caution and shyness. Abrupt stops are important telltale signs when you are evaluating a potential friend, lover, or marriage partner. It generally takes a lot of time to get close to such people.

The t-bar

"The t-bar has more significance than any other letter or grouping," writes a graphoanalyst. It is true that corresondence course graphoanalysis hinges on the t-bar. The variations are intriguing enough, as you will see, but in graphology the t-bar is only one small helpmate.

According to schools in the United States, a normal or average t-bar crossing should be three-fourths of the way up the stem as measured from the baseline. This indicates attainable goals by a person with average intelligence.

The strength of the t-bar helps determine to some extent a person's determination. The length tells us about willpower, enthusiasm and drive.

Some examples of strong, energetic, consistent t-bars are in Figures 61, 72, and 81. All these people (along with many others represented in the book) have enough willpower, determination, and drive, along with goal-orientation. It is logical from what we have already learned that the up-tilted t-bar indicates hope and optimism; the reverse applies to the downstroke. People with lofty ideals cross their t's high above the stem (sometimes so far above that they are obviously in a dream world). Pressure indicates action-prone vitality. A delicate bar appeals to the sensitive person, a low bar to the timid or humble. The absence of a t-bar means sloppiness, carelessness, rebelliousness or procrastination. The t-bar ahead of the stem achieves the dubious distinction of belonging to someone who knows what to do but does not do it.

Some writers cross their t's with a little knot. Here is a persistent (perhaps obstinate) person who will not give up easily. It can also be a sign of selfishness in a low FN. Other deceptive types employ such a long bar (see Figure 84), perhaps even a double bar, that the t-formation acts like a smoke screen that conceals the author's real intentions. (See Figure 83.)

Dagger-like designs with sharp points express sarcasm or bludgeoning callousness. Strongly curved umbrellas are associated with domineering individuals. Acquisitive hooks (Figure 45), cavemen with stones (the i-dot, Figure 17), and angular gallows-like forms (Figure 50) all offer fascinating variations of anti-social tendencies.

Lower Loops

Lower loops show us the sexual, physical, material area. Again a caveat: There has to be more supporting proof in the writing for whatever we see in the lower loops. In fact, it is quite feasible to write letters like g, p, y, and others with a simple, loopless downstroke.

The resolute straightness of the loopless downstroke can provide an insight into the writer's character. The firm, straight downstroke can plunge as deeply and as strongly into the earth (and into the physical world) as a farmer's spade. Other lower lengths (see the "f" in Figure 21) barely break the sod and can be uprooted easily. The writer of Figure 21 simply does not have a strong hold on life.

The absence of a loop in an otherwise strong plunge shows an absence of sexual or financial imagination and has nothing to do with character strength. Professional sports figures often write this way, expressing their interest in physical activity with powerful but loopless g's and y's. Other athletic people do use some loops.

An elegantly executed loop as part of an extra long lower extension (as in Figures 75 and 81) can indicate business talent and involvement with money. If the loops of these letters are wide (as in Figure 90), we must suspect the writer's special interest in sex. Very broad lower loops point to other pleasures—cooking or wine, for instance—whereas very tiny, atrophied loops (see Figure 78) are those of ascetic people, or at least of persons to whom sex, gourmet cooking, and sports mean very little.

Lastly, there are lower extensions, such as the "g's" in Figure 91, which express receptivity in all these areas. These loops show that the person is open to the world and ready to try new physical sensations. The exact opposite, a simple, staff-like g-extension, signals an individual who concentrates on other than the physical side of life.

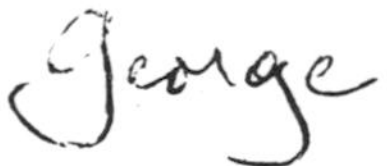

Figure 91.

Other Small Letters

Much can be seen in the small o's and a's. When written according to the copybook model, the o is a compact little oval connected to the next letter without a break. The o (as well as the a) offers a chance for variety, however. These letters can be tightly closed, or shut with a small loop, opened slightly, or wide open. (They may even be left open at the bottom.)

Few writers have the muscular control to form each letter precisely the same size, or in the same way, as the one before, so naturally there can be variations from one line to another. For this reason, you must determine the *average* graphic expression to arrive at your analysis.

It is common to leave a's or o's open at the top. Here is the candid and possibly talkative individual. If the letters are totally open in an otherwise unharmonious script, you may be dealing with someone who talks too much, who divulges too much information.

One of my colleagues compares the open a to "viewing an open mouth." Such a mouth, he says, "rattles and chatters." It follows, that the closed o or a is the choice of the less communicative individual—someone with whom you can share your personal affairs. (See "document" in Figure 45.)

It is possible to overdo the closure with a little knot at the top of the o. Depending on the FN and other indications, the knot formation characterizes the ability to keep a secret (and, in some cases, secretiveness). If there is not only a little loop but also a line, or a series of spirals, within the o, the person is not apt to be candid with anyone. Such closed individuals make poor friends. (There will be more about this in Chapter 6 on honesty.)

We mentioned the m's and n's elsewhere. It is worth repeating that garlands (open) letters, especially with a high FN in the script, express frankness, and arcaded (arch-like) m's are a sign of caution, a sense of etiquette, secretiveness, and inhibition, if there is other supportive graphic evidence. Finally, an m or n can be done with snake-like double curves that, at best, express adaptability and diplomacy; at worst, easy changeability and chameleon-like qualities.

Dotting the i's

It does not take a graphoanalyst (or a graphologist) to point out that a neat, carefully formed dot placed over the top of the i indicates a sense of order as does the t-bar placed horizontally at the midpoint of the t stem. Any school teacher can confirm that only the most negligent children leave off the i-dots altogether. But there are some variations that seem worth mentioning. How about the person who insists on employing a little circle above the i? Or the writer who uses a star? (See Figure 92.)

Figure 92.

Or why not an accent instead of a dot?

All of the above are simply people who strive for individuality. The woman in 92, for example, is a cabaret dancer, and it feels good to her to use a star, just as some movie stars do. The circle in Figure 48 is a young secretary's attempt to appear artistic.

The i-dot can also be placed very high, in the area of religion and idealism. Other writers carefully (punctually) dot the i ahead of the letter itself. An interesting departure from the norm is the intellectual's practical shortcut (see the "i" in the word "issue," Figure 93) which ties the dot in a line to the next letter (an "s" in this case).

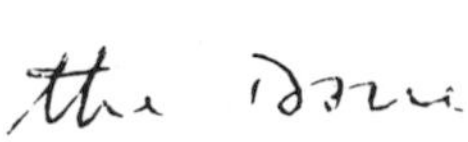

Figure 93.

The i-dot can also serve as a hook, which may have to do with attempts to get someone's attention, or with greed (in a materialistic script). As always, one must search for more evidence. Never make snap judgments.

6

Traits, Talents and Sexuality

If there is any one characteristic we value in others, surely it is honesty. The amateur graphologist will look for honesty in the writing of a prospective friend, companion, spouse or partner. We must pay the piper if we get involved with the insincere, the crooked or the criminal.

That is why the signs of straight-forwardness and the indicators of deceitful, phoney, or chronically dishonest persons should be on the agenda of every graphology student.

We say indicators, because a single negative observation would not suffice. Dr. Pulver and his peers always recommend that one search for at least three or four different indicators of dishonesty.

Honesty and Dishonesty

To be sure, it is not difficult to tell if a writer is straightforward. The trait shows up at once. How? The writing will be even and clear. Sincere people seldom adorn their scripts. The essentials do the job. There will not be any extreme shifts of direction or any compulsion to appear different. Nor do sincere, trustworthy people favor bizarre formations, graphic fireworks, illegibility, or the need to write very slowly to create special effects.

There are innumerable illustrations in this book. Examine Figures 8, 24, and 36. All are remarkably clear. The purity and absence of artificiality emerge in Figures 46 and 52. In the same vein, a brief glance at Figure 79 will show you a devoted nurse, a sterling character, a sincere human being. She does not aim for fancy capitals, does not change direction, and does not want to impress anyone.

The simplicity of such intelligent, cultured writers as are seen in Figures 61 and 64 goes hand in hand with an open, straightforward attitude. The latter also shows up in garlands, rather than arcades. (See Figure 46.) The writers avoid all grandiose gestures of exaggeration: excess decorations, complex strokes and various spiral formations.

This leads us to a look at the major expressions of the dishonest. Letters that should open at the top but have been changed by the writer and have hidden bottom openings are one expression. It is not easy to pry open the underside of an o in this manner, but it has been done. The a can be similarly operated upon, as can the g or y. (See the various illustrations in Figure 94.) The small b lends itself admirably to a concealed slit (see "above" in Figure 5) and the capital B proves ideal to such subterranean manipulations. (See "B" in Figure 95.) The writers of the capital "D" in "Denver" (Figure 96) and the "D" in "Dick" (Figure 87) are up to similar tricks. These openings are always regarded as *one* sign of dishonesty or hypocrisy, but we still need more evidence.

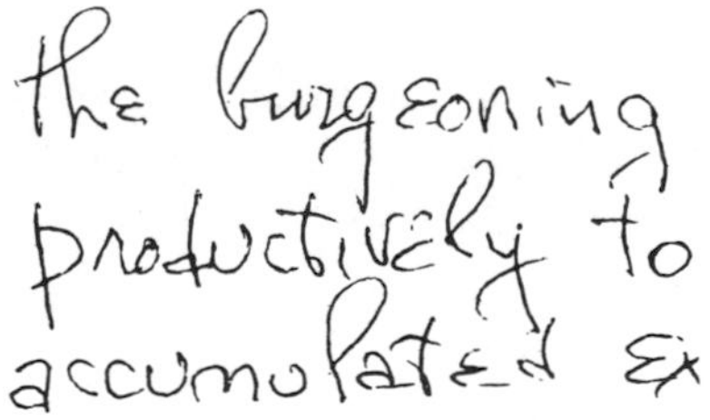

Figure 94.

Figure 95.

Figure 96.

Dr. Pulver warns that any spiderweb patterns, whether elegantly or clumsily done, should be distrusted. The eminent graphologist referred especially to the extra circles and turns inside small letters like an a (see Figure 97), as well as overdecorated capitals with many extra strokes, as in Figure 4.

Figure 97.

Too many hidden spiderwebs in an a (see Figure 97) always mean deceit in one form or another. (In a positive FN, the writer never learned how to be frank with someone else and therefore cannot be trusted.)

There are handwritings that may contain so many extra circles that we must suspect pathological liars. Others do their decorations with the verve of con men who are totally sure of themselves, in words and in writings.

Deliberate substitutions of letters are telltale signs of the dishonest. We do not refer to the rapid writing of the doctor's prescription, probably written for the 20th time: The physician's boredom results in letters that are unintentionally illegible. The dishonest person proceeds with legible falsifications, which is easy enough. You need only look at the use of the "S" instead of the "L" in Figure 98. (It should be "Lowell," not "Sowell.")

Figure 98.

There are countless other switches seen in the hands of embezzlers or crude criminal liars. Moreover, such people will exchange figures as well, substituting, for instance, a 3 for a 5.

Many expert graphologists also warn you against educated people who write at extremely slow speeds, manufacturing letters as they go along. One such case was the woman in Figure 48: The contrived angles themselves would be seen by Dr. Pulver as falseness. Such slow productions are not unusual for people who write a great deal, such as the author of Figure 31 whose premeditated extra strokes show a clever mind capable of all sorts of invented excuses.

The slow fabrication was also the hallmark of Figure 94, which we studied for its g's open at the bottom (this makes two counts of dishonesty). It should be emphasized that an uneducated farm laborer may also furnish a very slow sample, but with a difference. He makes no effort at beautifying or fabricating, as does the characteristically dishonest individual of Figure 48.

The Roman arch, or arcade, is always a sign of secretiveness, offering an interpretation of dishonesty in concert with the cool person's slant and a low FN. The exaggerated "m" in "confirm" (see Figure 31) is a good illustration of the slowly made arcade in a contrived script. There are an endless number of other arcade writers in this book: Many of these people exhibit signs of dishonesty. One of the most revealing (and graphologically compelling) samples was that of the famous female gun slinger in Figure 50. Study again this left-slanted psychopath whose arcades look as strong as prison bars. In addition, she has some deftly designed webs in certain letters like the "g" in line 1. This adds up to three dishonest signs.

The negative aspects of thready writing indicate that the writer may be elusive, insincere, or a liar. The thread writer moves at high speeds with snakelike lines that make the message as unclear as the individual letters. One of the most unforgettable examples was that of Henry Kissinger (Figure 62) who slithered along with all kinds of undecipherable Gothic towers and symbols and various pyramids on the horizon. One has to grant him much originality—indeed, brilliance—in the execution of his diplomatic thread writing. Master graphologist Anthony spoke of "duplicity" and other dishonest tendencies. Even if this were not the case in an international game renowned for falseness, Kissinger's angular threads at least show deceit—the kind that led to many lawsuits for wiretapping.

The thready, moody, changeable writing of Figure 80 is minor compared to Kissinger's. All the same, Figure 80 remains so unclear and sways so much from one side to another that the writer must be the type who makes false promises. The writer of Figure 80 is simply too weak, too unprincipled, and too untrustworthy to be taken at his or her word.

Figure 99.

Watch out for any formations of shielding or topping, or encircled words, often in the form of a lasso. The lasso or shield could appear in the signature (see Chapter 7) or in the writing itself. Such shields or circles must be considered for their concealment tendencies. The shield can consist of a bizarre elongated d (Figure 4 is worth studying), or it may appear as an unnecessarily long t-bar, swung backward as in Figure 83. The complex lassoing, fast-talking Figure 99 is most revealing for its extra lines. But it is the signature that offers the best chance to put up a smoke screen against dishonesty. To determine honesty in a script, you need at least three, or better still four, pieces of graphic evidence before passing judgment.

Stability

Next to honesty, potential marriage partners, employers, and business people look for stability in a handwriting. Look at the opposite: If you read the entire book, you will have no trouble determining an emotional character from an extreme slant to the right. We have seen samples of the overexcitable, the hysterical and the moody. The scripts of such people will swing wildly from one slant to the other, will show graphic derailments in upper and lower spheres, and will at once be obvious in their stormy inconsistency.

Unstable, changeable types will *vary* their capitals, trying out all kinds of different (and often changing) forms. This can be interesting and should be interpreted as versatility in a high FN. In a poor writing, though, inconsistency means instability. Unstable scripts show little rigidity and strength (see the loose Figure 80). They cannot be harmonious like the stable and balanced writers of Figures 36 and 44. The aforementioned nurse (Figure 79) typifies the unexcitable, reliable, consistent, patient person. In this writing there is no impatience, no impulsiveness, no excess. Such balanced people naturally make excellent employees. They can stay calm when the chips are down and can somehow manage others in a crisis.

Sexuality: Abnormal and Normal

There is nothing wrong with the individual who has little or no libido at all. A few divorced women, having once given birth, sometimes swear off sex altogether or at least show scant interest in it. Others, like the writers of Figures 21, 49, and 78, possess just enough sexuality to maintain a marriage or relationship. This emerges from the small lower loops in the above three (female) handwriting samples. As we have stated elsewhere, there are persons like the woman gun slinger in Figure 50 or the society woman in Figure 87 whose angular, loopless lower zones and unusual scripts illustrate an ability to sublimate their sexual drive; that is, to channel it into other areas.

The writer of Figure 50 cleverly plotted holdups instead, substituting brutal acts for normal sex. The older woman in 87, after a long marriage, began to concentrate on fashion, architecture, and party-giving with great success.

A weak sexuality shows up in tentative, shy, incomplete lower extensions like the "y" or "g" in Figure 76. A somehow unsatisfactory sexuality expresses itself in twisted, hooked, bizarre, and otherwise odd undercarriages, such as displayed in Figures 100, 101, and 102.

Figure 100.

Figure 101.

Figure 102.

All of the above individuals suffer from some sexual dysfunction, which can vary from frigidity or distaste to lack of control, anxieties, or partial impotence. These three samples are interesting, and they give us a chance for some other observations. For instance, the cold writer of Figure 101 leans into the most emotionless zone and then avoids all loops. This particular woman is far too reserved (see also the cut-off first letter) for a normal sexuality. The writer of Figure 102, apart from her typically spinsterish "y," lets her capital "M" (the ego) stand so far apart from the rest of the word (the opposite sex) that there could never be good rapport. The male writer of Figure 103 does not have any sexual problems except for a certain amount of "macho" pugnaciousness, which might be expected from a former cop and professional boxer. He is a good man, but he would be mismatched with a delicate woman.

How about 104? The triangular loop is that of an aggressive personality. This woman would make a poor choice for a timid, sexually fearful male.

Lastly, Figure 105 was selected for its healthy sexual expression. Other such examples appear throughout this book.

Figure 103.

Figure 104.

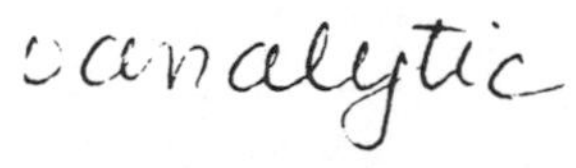

Figure 105.

For example, look once more at the writing of Rita R. (Figure 13), which has been analyzed in depth. In addition to the solid lower loops, Rita favors an affectionate slant, which always is a sign of good sexual relations. She is a passionate woman. The dancer of Figure 92 has a healthy, energetic libido; and you may remember the large loops in Figure 90, which pictorialized a strong sexual drive.

At this point it should be mentioned that we must always look for graphic proportions. A tiny script may come with tiny loops as well; their size is in perfect accord with the rest of the writing. Age comes into play, too; always ask for it. Expect less libido from a 60-year-old man than from a youth of twenty. Lastly, constantly changing loops suggest a changeable sexuality, dependent on one's mood.

Generosity and Kindness

If the left to right movement symbolizes the bridge from the me to the you, then we must look for generosity in handwriting width. The giving writer generally does not mind wasting a little paper. He or she prefers wide connections between letters, and reaches out with the terminal strokes. (Some generous people also have large scripts.)

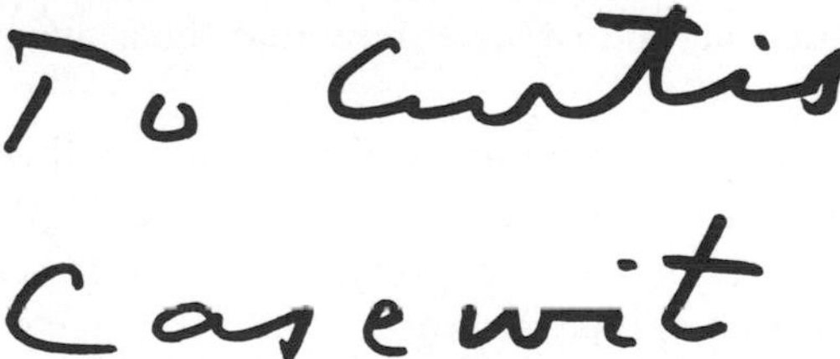

Figure 106.

Recall that Rita R. (Figure 13) had wide strokes and reached out at the ends of many words. Largesse can often be seen in extra large, round handwriting just as pettiness emerges from the microscopic, angular, sharp hand. Generosity teams up with kindness if a script is consistently curved and round like that of Figure 46, for instance, *and* has wide connections. The writer of Figure 46 illustrates two other graphologically positive points: 1) she writes with great speed and hence is naturally spontaneous and generous, and 2) her writing leans in an affectionate way that symbolizes warmth. (See also the generous writing of Paul de Ste. Colombe in Figure 106.)

To be sure, slowly manufactured width, perhaps with angular and geometric patterns like Figure 107, has the opposite connotation. Here is a calculating, false person who merely wants to appear generous and giving but always considers the giving of a gift from a purely personal viewpoint.

Figure 107.

The same must be said for many strokes that return selfishly to the ego, like Figure 75, whose stand-off capitals show that she is always number one in any transaction.

Finally, there are only rare cases of people with writing too tight to be truly generous (see Figure 49), because tightness implies fear, increased control, inhibitions, and caution, all enemies of truly selfless acts. This is not to say that Figure 49 types cannot be kind: Compressed handwriting *can* be round and amiable.

Artistry and Musical Sense

A famous architect once explained that "less is more," thus praising simplicity in the arts. He attacked *Kitsch* and its heaped-on decorations. The same often applies to your diagnosis of artistry in someone's handwriting. The truly gifted commercial artist, the book publishing art director, the well-known architect, and the famous painter all write simply. (One need only recall Picasso's sparse signature.) Artistic gifts and the understanding of art produce writing such as in Figure 108 (note the simple "T" and the design of the "th") or the distinctive letter "f" in 109. In fact, creativity shows up in the creation of new letters and capitals, along with a harmonious use of space. A writer who crams a message into a corner casts doubt on his or her artistic talent and taste. On the other hand, the society woman of Figure 87 is also a patron of the arts, which is not astonishing considering the superb arrangement of her well-balanced letter. (Note the location of the name on top.) It is worth returning to Figure 8 for its simple beauty, or to study Figure 36 for its arrangement. You will find many such pleasing graphic pictures in the book.

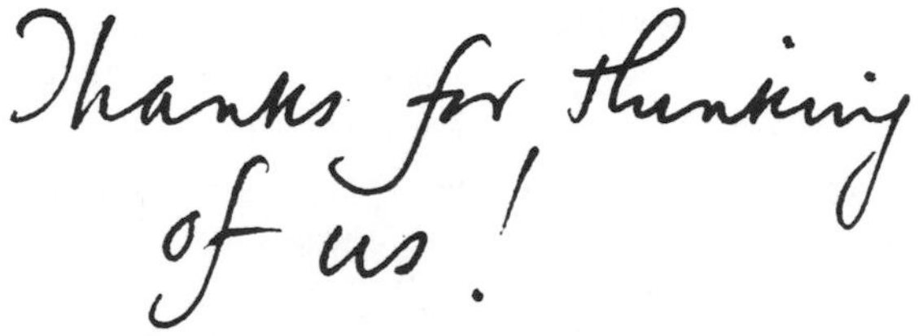

Figure 108.

Figure 109.

How about musical talents? Please note that some people possess them without ever using them; others just enjoy music. According to Dr. Pulver, musically involved people (or lovers of music) may elect to use musical symbols such as the clef-like "f" in Figure 108. (Beethoven actually used musical notes instead of the d, as did some of his contemporaries.) I have found that all truly musical people write with a sense of rhythm, repeating the beat of each line, seldom making erratic stops. Their writing flows like that in Figure 61, one of many examples.

Naturally, composers and long-time soloists reveal themselves in other ways as well. These musicians will write with slants that betray great feeling. After all, music is mainly emotion, as pianist Arthur Rubenstein often told us. A glance at Beethoven's writing will confirm that statement. The emotions need not all be positive ones: a great sense of despair or anger may produce musical handwritings.

Intelligence

Psychologists define intelligence in many ways and there are indeed many kinds of intelligence. A quick grasp of facts, powers of concentration, clarity of mind, elimination of superfluous information, and openness all help. This is perhaps why so many of the world's great minds write with a minimum of flourish, sticking to the essentials instead. Their analytical minds express themselves in fairly small, modest scripts, sometimes with sharp corners. Their sense of organization becomes obvious, as for example, is the organization seen in Figure 36, the script of a leading educator.

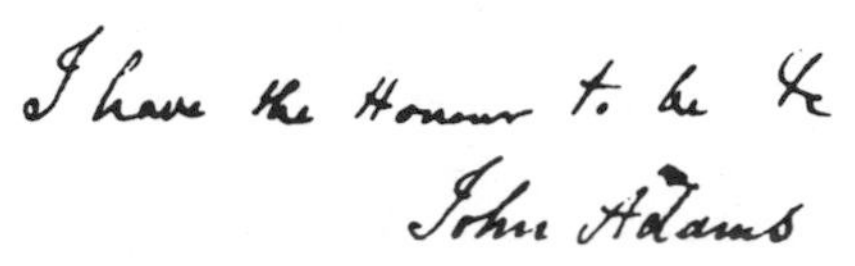

Figure 110.

Interestingly, some of the most brilliant historical figures, like John Adams, who signed the Declaration of Independence, wrote with a disarming clarity. In Figure 110, note how Adams' critical faculties express themselves in the angular "m" and "n." The lines are always apart and the words are fully spaced. The message is legible. Again, such intelligent persons will depart from the school norm and come up with some modifications in their writing, like the sharp "J" in John Adams' sample. You may wish to study other well-organized and individualized specimens that have appeared in previous chapters. For example, there is the intellectually well-connected "Th" in Figure 87, the triangular "A" in Figure 61, and the "I" in Figure 52, which typify an intelligent hand.

The Scientist

The connective line that may include the h linked to a T and the i-dot flowing into other letters, often characterizes the fluent mind of the scientist. Most handwriting of the great names—say, Einstein or Pasteur—are amazingly small, a sign of attention to detail and concentration. Nor is it an accident that major scientific talents in the fields of physics, chemistry, and medicine prefer the straight slant. The reason is simple enough. These people must be, above all, objective. They do not get into the passionate, subjective problems of slant writers. Patience is one of the cornerstones of their makeup and they finish a word to perfection. They cannot afford to be victims of capricious moods. Only seldom do scientists use pompous or decorative penmanship meant to impress others.

Health Versus Illness

Figure 111.

Figure 112.

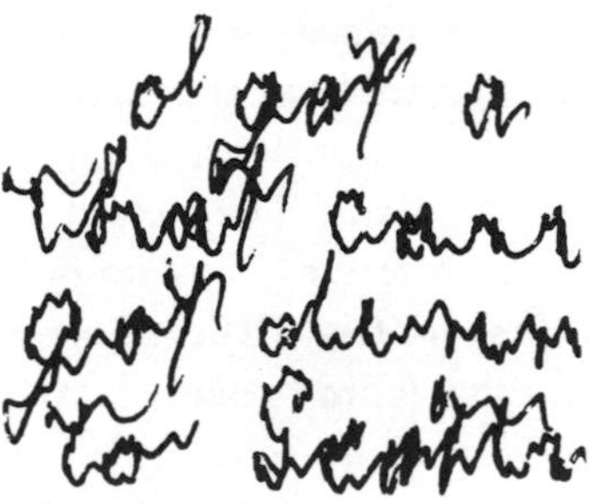

Figure 113.

What do the preceding three specimens have in common? They were all written by people afflicted with physical illness. Figure 111, which should be studied under a magnifying glass, belongs to a young man recovering from a recent heart attack. A careful analysis reveals the trembling execution of the "t" and "g."

The specimen in Figure 112 is the signature of Franklin D. Roosevelt, who suffered from the effects of infantile paralysis. It is difficult to read. The example in Figure 113 clearly illustrates the debility and loss of neuromuscular control affecting an 80-year-old man. The script is tremulous, almost as if the thread of life is running out. The man died shortly afterward.

Experienced graphologists emphasize that even lesser disorders—in fact, the slightest malaise—bring about changes in penmanship. Dr. H.O. Teltscher, a leading U.S. expert in disease and graphodiagnosis, explains.

> It is obvious that handwriting is affected by any pathological changes of an organ that interfere with the normal, regular functioning of the central or peripheral nervous system. Also, physical ailments that cause mechanical disturbances of movements will naturally find expression in handwriting. There are a number of variations that would seem to point to the existence of such organic disturbances—for instance, broken letters and loops, sudden extreme pressures on parts of letters only, to "fall down" constantly, and jerky or ragged letter formations.

All of this makes sense, of course, and there is plenty of graphic evidence. You need only compare the last three specimens with the scores of healthy ones in this book. It pays to study the changing script of a seriously ill family member. A fractured letter, a tremulous line, and other problems show up very quickly.

Emotional Problems

The same applies to emotional troubles; a slight neurosis, a psychosis, a deep depression, a nervous breakdown, or mental aberrations. Much work has been done by Dr. Teltscher and others in determining severe cases of schizophrenia. An extremely interesting study on the subject was also done by Dr. D.B. Douglas, a New York neurologist, with the help of D. Sara, a graphologist. The team came up with a helpful list of handwriting characteristics of schizophrenics. Among them are:

Abnormal underlining and overlining
Exaggerated ornamentation
Overall decay
Distortion of individual forms
Constant zone shifts
Contraction alternating with expansion
Splitting of individual letters
Unduly abrupt or involved movement components
Explosive unevenness in zones, baseline, and letter endings
Bizarre forms

Dr. Teltscher's research (backed by my own) also unearthed extreme cases with lines running into one another, such as is seen in Figure 114. The pattern here is so extreme that even a novice can see the loss of contact with the normal world. The lines are going in every direction. The writer has lost all sense of reality. The wildness of this picture also suggests hysteria.

Figure 114.

Graphology is equally useful in the diagnosis of other major mental disturbances. Dr. Teltscher states: "Increasing illegibility in scripts that were formerly clear and legible, coupled with increasing irregularities in writings that once were regular, gives warning that mental imbalance may be gradually developing." Other typical signs are: "frequent omission of letters or syllables, varying slants, and lines that swing in various directions."

Dr. Teltscher also made a detailed list of graphic symptoms found among the emotionally disturbed. He suggests that you watch for the following:

> Different slants—right, vertical, and backward slants may be seen in one specimen; varying pen pressure, all the way from fine to heavy or muddy writing; different ways of crossing the t's, from firm t-bars to none at all; lines that waver and vacillate; letters inharmoniously shaped; stress on nonessential features; capitals unusually flourished; lower loops too small or too large or neglected altogether; leftward tendencies very often; indistinct and clear words in one line; microscopically small writings that show narrowness; cramped and compressed letters; the single words are isolated from one another; and, finally, threadlike structure.

It stands to reason that some of the above descriptions, especially the wavering and vacillating, apply to chronic alcoholics or certain drug addicts. Both excessive liquor and drugs like LSD have a destructive effect on our ability to write well, to stick to a line, and to shape clear, steady letters. The opposite is also true. When you see a well-ordered, superbly balanced, harmonious script, such as in Figure 115, you know you are dealing with a physically and emotionally intact person, in this case a young man aged 25. He is a person who has it together.

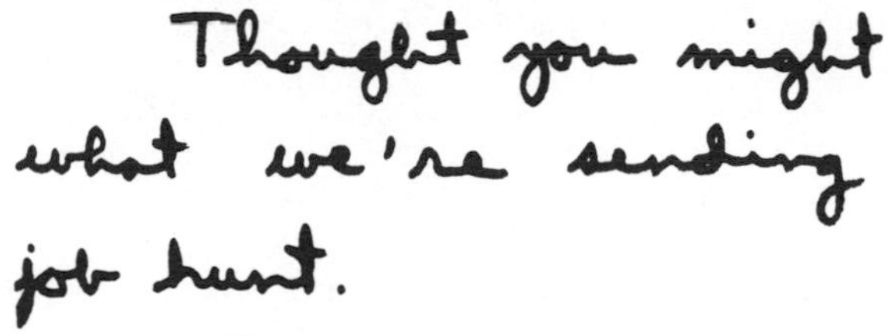

Thought you might
what we're sending
job hunt.

Figure 115.

This person has none of the rhythmic disorders described by Dr. Teltscher and none of the many graphic signs that can be diagnosed as abnormal. My own collection of samples also points to excessive spirals, as we saw in Figure 97, or constant mistakes and corrections as signs of severe conflicts. (Such graphic expressions must occur in many samples over a long period of time.) Severely depressed people write in sinking lines, just as hallucinating types use the steeply climbing direction. Dr. Pulver's listings of neurotic personalities include those who do a *Spiegelschrift*, which means "mirror writing" (see Figures 116, 117).

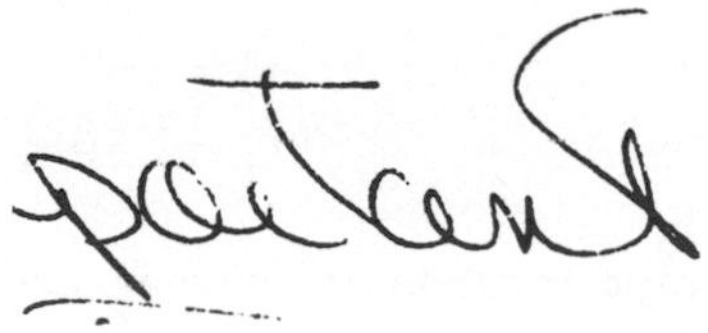

Figure 116.

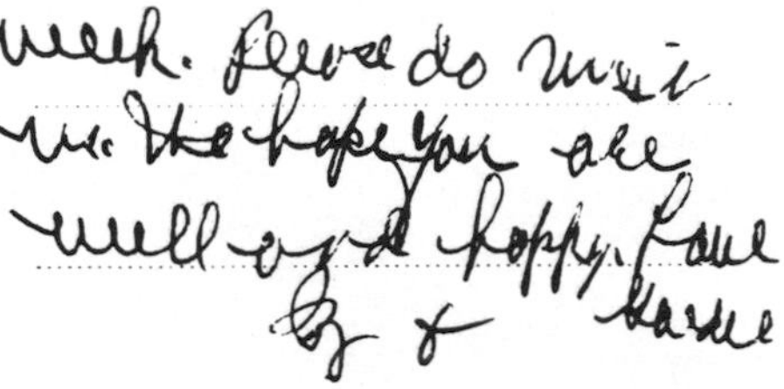

Figure 117.

Nervous exhaustion and other nervous conditions express themselves in swaying, formless, illegible scripts like Figure 70 or Figure 80. Some writers are hardly able to form a single letter without a break, so that each word looks like an X-ray of a comminuted bone fracture. To be sure, any writing that seems scattered across the page, changes direction willy nilly, *and* always separates caps from words, belongs to a person with strong inner conflicts and withdrawal symptoms. A typical sample appears below in Figure 118.

Figure 118.

Note the queer isolated caps, the direction change, and the distance between the words. All are significant symptoms for the alienated, hypersensitive individual.

There are also the maladjusted loners, the fearful, anxiety-ridden, dejected people who somehow manage to get along nevertheless. Psychiatrists estimate that there must be millions of Americans with the above problems, but they do not seek help, for personal reasons. The pressure of our society to succeed is misery for such people. They do not need hospitalization, but their unhappy state expresses itself in their handwritings. Among them is the crushed (but still trying) spinster in Figure 88; the woman of Figure 117 who has a low self-image (see lines through "W" in "We"), the bubbly show-off (Figure 86), the sexually active (Figure 78), and the dissatisfied "Mary" in Figure 102.

By contrast, a strong, secure handwriting like so many throughout these pages radiates its strength in every word and line. One recent example was that of Figure 115, a young man who shows serene strength, self-confidence and patience.

7

Signatures

A signature is a microcosm of the whole handwriting. A signature reflects all the traits and underlines the major ones. To be sure, we can apply everything we have learned about the Formniveau or writing quality to the autograph. We can scrutinize it for slant, speed, accuracy, size, pressure, and use of space. Moreover, we can look for boldness or acknowledge meekness. We can see whether the writer is spontaneous or cautious, arrogant or modest, open or concealing. All of the rules apply; however, as mentioned before, we should demand more handwriting samples and avoid looking at the signature per se, if we can help it. At times, of course, the signature is all we have.

The signature is part of the whole and at the same time a poster. "This is me!" the signature calls out. "This is how I want to be seen and known." So it is little wonder that the famous personages in history—the kings, princes, and generals—often had enormous signatures. They aimed for a picture of greatness.

Discrepancy between Handwriting and Signature

It is important to compare how someone signs a name to a letter and then study the letter itself. Are the sizes the same? If the capitals are proportionate, the signer is truly modest and sees no reason for conceit or arrogance. He or she is the same in public and in private. If someone signs with flourish and a much larger signature than the writing itself, you can be sure of one thing: The writer wants to project a successful, important image, despite personal limitations. A typical example appears below. In Figure 119 the writer wants to give the impression of great success and power, a fact not borne out by the small humble script.

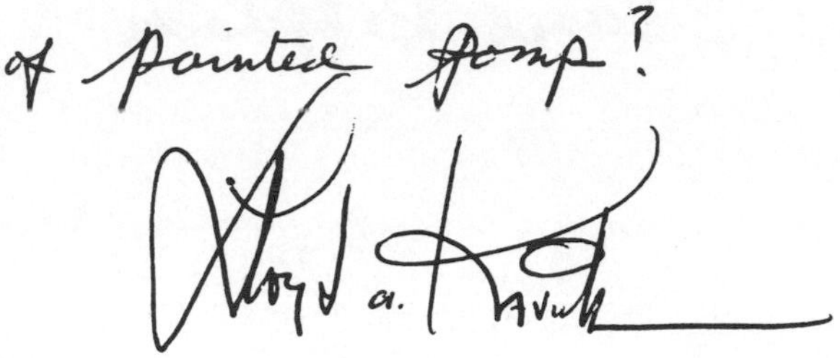

Figure 119.

Certainly there are personalities who are daring and dynamic. A typical one is that of Fred Praeger (Figure 120) a well-known publisher, whose bold, innovative "P" really stands out.

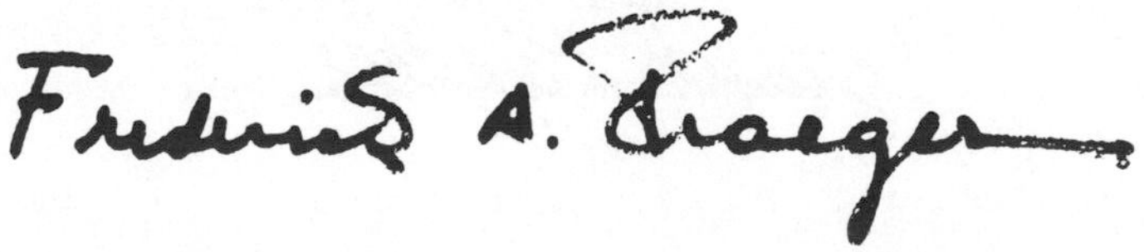

Figure 120.

The signature represents the public image and the main body of the script represents what one really is like. Figure 121 makes this point. The graphologist recognizes here a man who is aware of his own intelligence, taste and artistic gifts. His outer appearance (the signature) tallies with his self-image (the writing).

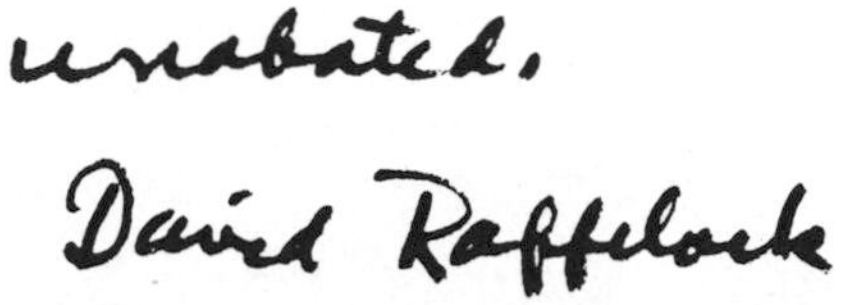

Figure 121.

In the same sense, the "Frank Kappler" in Figure 122 is only slightly larger than his "Best regards." It means that this energetic, outgoing resort association executive wants to appear sure of himself. This is understandable for a somewhat young man who, if he did not project poise, would not be taken seriously.

Figure 122.

Kappler's script illustrates other features, such as the optimistically climbing line, and the carefully stretched out hand at the end of the name. His simple, effective, efficient "F" is that of an executive who has learned to organize his time.

Keep in mind that if the script is large, but the signature is small, the writer prefers a different projection: He wants to appear humble. In the meantime, the large script shows his true opinion of himself.

Such discrepancy between the official and the private also extends to the slant. A person may use a backhand slant when penning the name, showing an official position of aloofness, and then write privately with an affectionate lean. Such backhand or at least straight signatures seem understandable when you sign a completely unimportant check. Surely, there is no need to appear affectionate when paying the plumber. Many people deal with accountants, tax collectors, and other strangers in a neutral manner, just as their signatures may slant lovingly when corresponding with their children (in a letter that shows that they are normally cool.

Underlining

All the rules concerning oversized caps with small middle zones apply to signatures, too. One excellent example is Figure 123, that of Jacqueline Kennedy Onassis. It is almost self-explanatory. Her oversized capitals mirror gross conceit and a huge vanity.

The "d" is made to appear sexy, a fact belied by the slow, unspontaneous, over-controlled backhand script. Her "K" not only stands snobbishly alone but also expresses a pushy, ruthless, know-it-all personality, whose curt final "y" shows how she has always treated the press. The arcaded "n's" are those of a secretive woman.

Figure 123.

She does not underline her signature because its size is self-important enough, taking up a great deal of room. Many writers, including this one, (Figure 124) do underline their names. They want to make it clear that they consider themselves important in their fields or professions. Apart from authors, professors, executives, and architects, actors of many countries use the single underlining stroke such as in Figure 124. One other illustration is Figure 125, a well-known ski racer.

Figure 124.

Figure 125.

Some personalities in business (or the field of entertainment—see Figure 92) use part of their name for underscoring, an easy thing to do for dancer Carmen Holiday. When I asked her why she did it, she said she first saw the "C" used like this in a Coca Cola sign. There are people who content themselves with a single small line under their names (see Figure 126, a TV personality).

Others do not find it necessary to underline. One example was furnished earlier by John Adams (Figure 110) whose extraordinary simplicity for one so powerful was combined with a sharp, analytical mind.

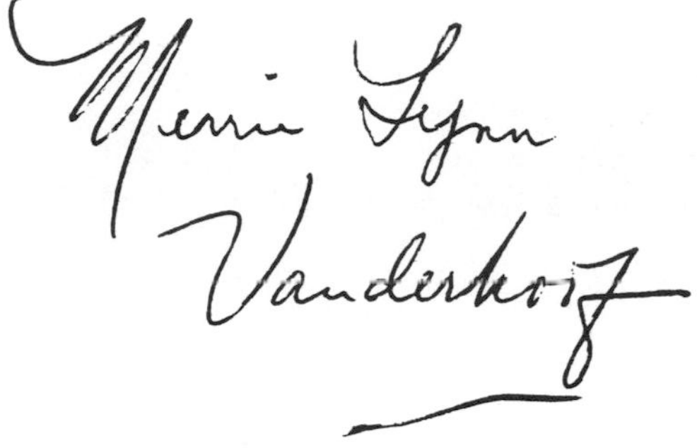

Figure 126.

To be sure, smallness and the absence of an underscore is no guarantee of a positive analysis. A simple signature can undulate uncertainly (see Figure 127, for instance). The signature denotes a lack of self-confidence or inner strength. It shows (via the three caps) inadequate communication with and fear of other people, moodiness, and insecurity (see the peevish sting of the "M"). On the positive side, the sensitivity can be a useful trait for a creative worker.

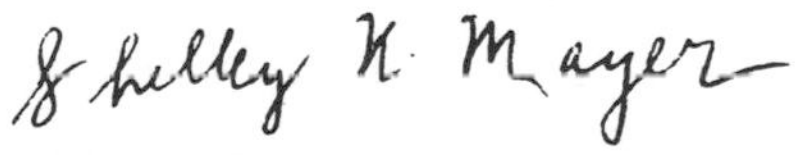

Shelley K. Mayer

Figure 127.

Things to Look For in an Autograph

It should be emphasized that many autographs repeat features you may have noticed in the writing itself. You will thus find that the slow-moving, self-conscious, chronically depressed writer of Figure 82 also exhibits these traits in her writing. The line goes down at a visible angle; she pauses after every capital (the ego expression); and she moves slowly, with every stroke being completed, school-fashion.

Some people sign so many letters that they must simplify the autograph. Figure 128 is a typical illustration.

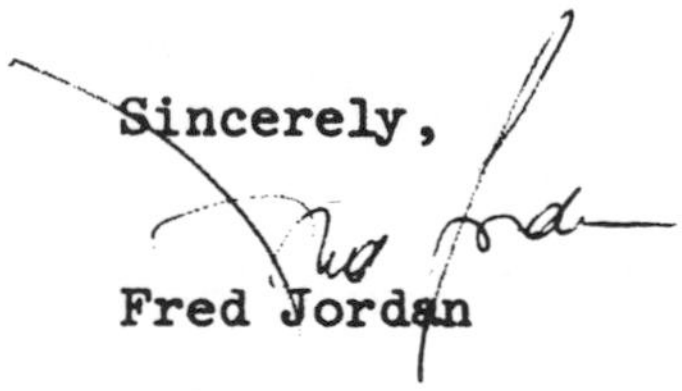

Sincerely,

Fred Jordan

Figure 128.

Here letters are contracted and otherwise abbreviated. FDR (Figure 112) also is a good example of this tendency. Even before his illness FDR had to leave out some strokes to save time.

It is true that all the rules regarding loops, upper or lower, apply to the signature. The beautifully expanded sail-like caps in Figure 129 show this well enough.

They mirror a person who always uses large upper loops. The latter

JOHN A. LOVE

Figure 129.

were always a symbol for a fine imagination. The tapering off at the end of the name, if repeated elsewhere, indicates psychological talents, as in the case of novelist James Baldwin (Figure 130).

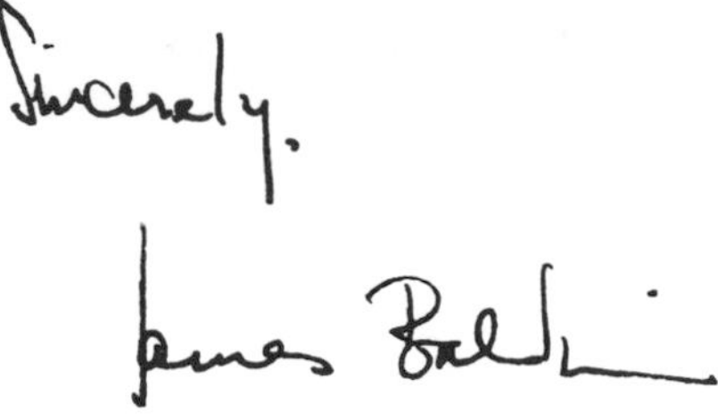

Figure 130.

Studies have shown that the sharp, stinging, aggressive angles and points of Figure 131 characterize the highly critical, competitive, sometimes irritable person. Figure 131 offers a significant example of the overscore: The last name, including the capital, is completely roofed in; the cover is done with special skill over the "A." Such sheltering umbrellas can be constructed by means of t and other letters. Some writers roof in their entire name, or even find a way to encircle it. What is the significance of this stroke?

It is explained briefly elsewhere: It always indicates secrecy; the writer does not want you to look into his or her cards. Many diplomats write this way, as do publishers, industrialists, inventors, and politicians.

Figure 131.

Figure 132.

The encirclement or umbrella-formation does not *necessarily* imply dishonest undercover transactions, but some less than savory behavior cannot be ruled out. (There must be at least two or three other graphic proofs of dishonesty.)

The signature seems ideal to the type of concealed, underhanded writing of Figure 132, just as the finale of an autograph lends itself to the sharp materialistic hook shown in Figure 133. It belongs to an historic figure who lived from 1735 to 1777. In fact, he was born the same year as the Harvard-trained patriot named John Adams. But Button Gwinnett, although a co-signer of the Declaration, was a different man altogether.

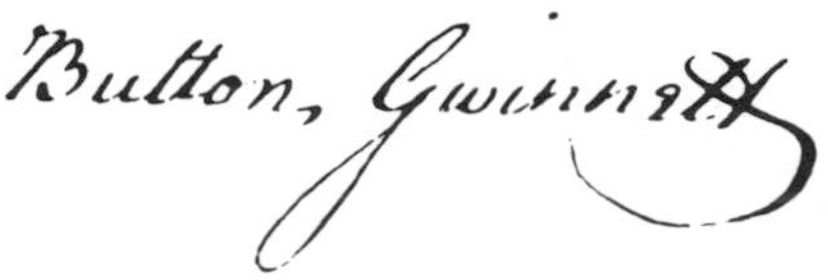

Figure 133.

Daniel Anthony, our finest American graphologist, called Gwinnett a "devious money-grabber" and a "slave-owning land speculator." Such inclinations emerge clearly in the overlong money-grasping capital "G," in the t-bars that almost represent dollar signs, and in the terminal scythe, a sharp rapacious hook that resembles the curved, pointed tool used by icemen. The slowly executed design of the small letters ties in with a calculating nature.

Such important symbols creep easily into a man's signature. Rolled-in caps (Figure 134) and other signs of selfishness also pop up with regularity.

Figure 134.

Some characteristics can occur only in someone's autograph. A protective shield behind the end of the name may be one of these. Observe the way some married women sign a document or letter. She may make the first name large. She may emphasize her maiden name and play down her husband's. Both instances may cast some doubt on the happiness or importance or her marriage. On the other hand, a woman who likes being married generally shows it by unconsciously stressing her married name.

The Signature Illustrating One Man's Life

It stands to reason that an individual's development—the rise and fall of a public figure, for instance—becomes visible via a series of signatures.

Graphologists have examined both Hitler's and Napoleon's

signatures and found much deterioration. Dr. Felix P. Lehmann, well-known Manhattan graphologist, charted the history of power-hungry Richard Nixon from the earliest days of his career to Watergate, when he almost destroyed our democracy, to his shameful resignation. The 1959 signature was given to the reporters who accompanied him to the American Trade Exposition in Moscow, where he became embroiled with Khruschev in the famous "Kitchen Debate." The letters are quite clear with good pressure and large capitals. They show Nixon as President Eisenhower's Vice President, working with energy, diligence, and purpose at the fulfillment of his enormous ambitions. According to Lehmann, Nixon's election in 1969 already brought change from a graphological standpoint. The initials are now out of proportion to the rest of the letters, which have lost much of their clarity. "Richard" is more pronounced than "Nixon." The "R" reaches into the stratosphere. Here is a man glorying in his personal success, which dwarfs his nondescript family. The now thready last name ties in with the new Nixon personality.

Lehmann writes: "He makes himself intentionally unclear to allow room for maneuvering and room for diplomacy deception. Angularity has crept in, denoting harshness and restlessness. In short: the president puts his personal ambitions and pride above the common welfare and rules with reckless deception. His signature gives an unaesthetic, ugly impression."

Lehmann next analyzed a signature of Nixon in the midst of the Watergate cover-up. It was wishy-washy; everything in a flux of ambiguity. Hiding things had become Nixon's second nature. The "R" and the end stroke of "Nixon" protect him from all sides: No one could come close to his secrets because of his distrust. "His self-confidence is shaken, he has become insecure, but he hopes to succeed with bluff and bluster to ride out the gathering storm. The structure of his signature is still intact."

The last signature was written shortly before his resignation. Lehmann described the pathetic picture of a man who had lost everything, and it evokes pity. The i-dot had become a check mark turned upside down, turned against him, a symbol of the investigations that threatened his very being. "There is nothing left, only a shadow. His ambitions are over. A shapeless stroke, a disintegration of personality, a person sinking within himself, engulfed and drowning under waves of unsufferable tensions." The scrawl gives the impression of a man racing to his doom: His St. Helena is coming up. Lehmann states: "The last signature has a melancholy fluidity, a kind of harmony letting it go the way it wants to, exhausted, ready to resign and die."

Some Signatures

Not many autographs evoke such dramatic remarks, or trace a man's demise. Some signatures contain a great measure of positive qualities. You will thus find it easy to tell much about Eugene Fodor, famous travel guide author and his colleague Arthur Frommer (Figures 135 and 136). Both are sales geniuses and, in Fodor's case, we must marvel at the elegant loops and connections that suggest Fodor's Hungarian charm. It is remarkable how much energy, direction, and sheer optimism radiate from this autograph; after all, Fodor is in his seventies. Frommer's "Arthur" is a more ambitious, a more bombastic style, but also daring, dynamic and brainy.

Figure 135.

Figure 136.

Test your own knowledge and grasp of the rules against a number of signatures (Figures 137 through 149) in Chapter 8. All of them are interesting and good analytical material. As with the overall analysis, concenrate on the gestalt first. Look at the form level, the quality. Search for harmony or confusion, accuracy or carelessness, speed or slowness. Pick out the most compelling characteristics, and only then focus on details. We will let you be the diagnostician.

Figure 137.

Erwin Knoll, Editor

Figure 138.

Evan Thomas

Figure 139.

Jeffrey R. Hills

Figure 140.

Figure 141.

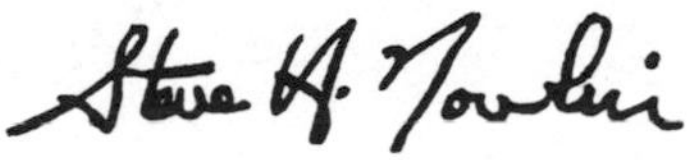

Figure 142.

Figure 143.

Figure 144.

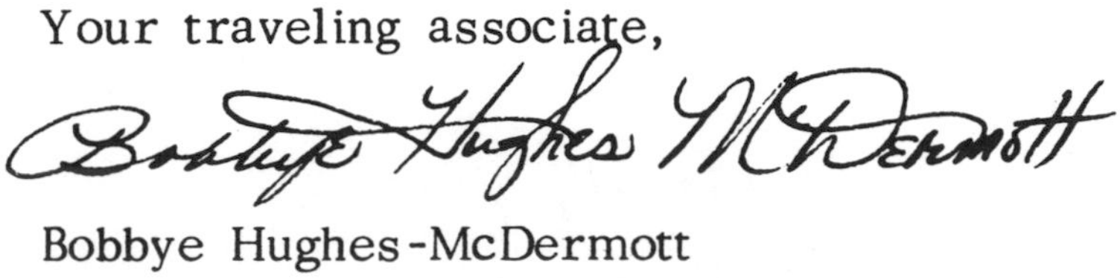

Your traveling associate,

Bobbye Hughes-McDermott

Figure 145.

Figure 146.

Figure 147.

Figure 148.

Figure 149.

8

Analyzing a Stranger's Handwriting

From what you have learned up to now, hopefully you will be able to analyze the handwriting of someone you have never met before. You already know that you need an adequate sample (in this case four partial lines), written quickly under optimum conditions (with a suitable pen, at a table), and written under normal circumstances (no traumatic states; no alcohol or drugs). We assume that the writer is right-handed; if not, we should be informed that the person uses the left hand.

If the writer is not present, you are entitled to ask for:

1) gender
2) age
3) nationality
4) profession

In the case of Figure 150, we are looking at the script of an American woman, aged 45. Ideally, the specimen of her writing should include margins, which were deleted because of space limitations. For the most accurate analyses, you need samples from various recent periods to see if you have the person's normal writing. (Temporary illness would change it, of course.) A signature is always desirable (in the case omitted) as a tool to underline any discrepancies and to mirror someone's self-image.

The experienced graphologist can work up a good analysis by

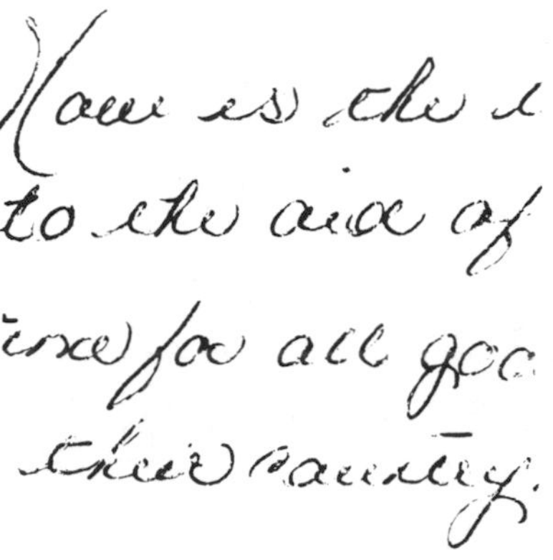

Figure 150.

making a few notes and then elaborating on the findings in writing. The newcomer, however, would be wise to proceed systematically along the lines of this book and note down the specifics that were mentioned in earlier chapters.

A true interest in people and a sense of observation are important, along with an ability to remember the many variations we discussed. A magnifying glass and good lighting are essential, too.

Let us attempt to catalogue Figure 150 in simple terms, as in this book, beginning with the handwriting quality.

Formniveau: The FN is above average because of line separations, consistency of letters, a good repetitive rhythm, excellent balance, and superior use of white space.

Even versus Uneven: This woman's script is remarkably even, which shows steadiness, mental balance, sturdy health, strength of purpose, and reliability.

Tempo: The writing is slow, there are no abbreviations, the pen does not race, and the letters do not smear. Deliberate writing such as this (along with other signs, like detached caps) shows extreme caution. She thinks before she acts. The slow penmanship aims for artistic forms, suggesting interest in the arts.

Slant: A slightly inclined slant shows that she can be affectionate.
Size: This somewhat large script shows a person who needs space and likes personal attention from others. The enormous capital (repeated elsewhere in her script) indicates extreme self-esteem bordering on arrogance. (Note the isolated "N.") This is an intelligent but opinionated person.
Zones: Both upper and lower zones are well developed. The lower zone, however, is emphasized by the clawlike downward end curve in the "y" of "country." This is a symbol for strong, greedy materialism. The capital "N" looms in the same zone. In this regard, Figure 150 reminds one somewhat of Figure 133.
Connections: These are the well-linked letters of a logical, smooth-thinking person. Strong welding points to strength of character to the point of stubborness. A disconnected cap points to snobbishness (combined with size).
Arcades and Garlands: Combinations of these with sharp angles, that can be diagnosed as critical ability.
Rigidity: Here is a major hallmark of this writing. Its significance is that this woman will not budge from her viewpoint nor adapt herself to others. She will not give in.
Pressure: Strong, energetic, decisive pressure.
Loops: There are no extremes in the loops.

Many graphologists make a work sheet, noting down the various emerging traits. The primary ones are:

Materialism (acquisitiveness)
Rigidity (will not adapt herself)
Steadiness
Caution

And the remaining traits are:

Mental balance
Good health
Strength
Affectionate
Needs space
Needs admiration
Extreme self-esteem (arrogance)
Snobbishness

Logical
Critical ability
Stubborn
Energetic

There are some schools of thought that suggest measuring the slant and size of a handwriting and the distance between words to arrive at a verdict. Some practitioners use rulers and other paraphernalia, drawing lines in various inks through a script, and so on.

Daniel Anthony and his students employ a well thought-out graphological psychogram (see Figure 151) for the purpose of summing up all the observed patterns. The chart includes all the items that we listed for analyzing Figure 150, along with all sorts of other details that are not always available. (Margins, for instance, are of little help on postcards, and covering strokes—item 28 in the chart—need not be present.) Most of my European colleagues simply work from notes.

The final step is to put all the personality facets together, combining the traits in your written report. It could be one to two pages, or longer. (For a sample, see Rita R.'s analysis in Chapter 1.)

Literary skills become useful. Daniel Anthony's style can be seen below in his descriptions of some well-known public figures.

> *Subject A:* His decency toward the press and the public is suggested by the sensitive and embracing response one gets from the tender and tiny curvatures of the linking letters and contacting strokes forming his signature. Given half a chance, he could be a kind and good man. His intention is always to be fair and judicious, honest and direct, but he has learned to roll with the punches.
>
> *Subject B:* The shortened signature projects a facile and functional man who has learned to think before he speaks.
>
> *Subject C:* Pedestrian, prosaic, unimaginative, a conformist who deals with conventional problems in rigid, unbending, and frequently inflexible ways.
>
> *Subject D:* His handwriting conjures up a man in turmoil, torn between dreams of being a masterful executive and doubts about his ability to lead his corporate empire. A smooth salesman who knows how to make a sophisticated presentation of his assets. But that makes the inner man.

GRAPHOLOGICAL PSYCHOGRAM

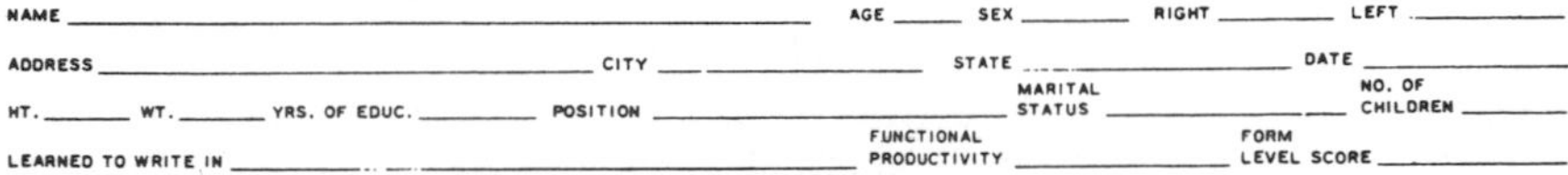
NAME ______ AGE ____ SEX ____ RIGHT ____ LEFT ____

ADDRESS ______ CITY ______ STATE ______ DATE ______

HT. ____ WT. ____ YRS. OF EDUC. ____ POSITION ______ MARITAL STATUS ______ NO. OF CHILDREN ____

LEARNED TO WRITE IN ______ FUNCTIONAL PRODUCTIVITY ______ FORM LEVEL SCORE ______

COUNTRY OR STATE

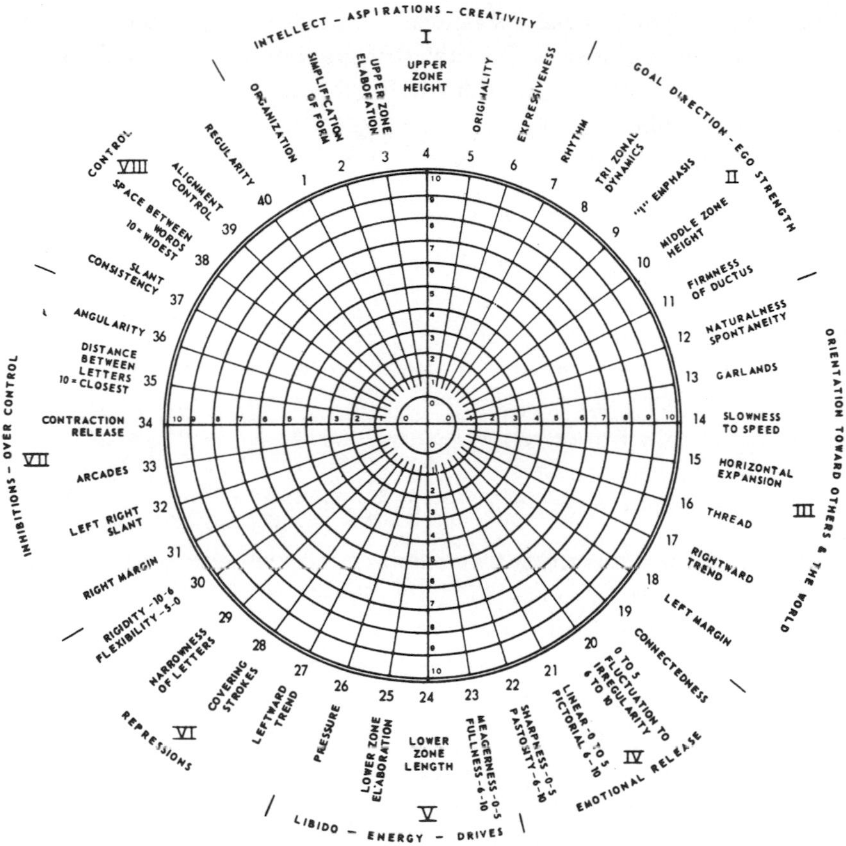

I INTELLECT – ASPIRATIONS – CREATIVITY
1 ORGANIZATION
2 SIMPLIFICATION OF FORM
3 UPPER ZONE ELABORATION
4 UPPER ZONE HEIGHT
5 ORIGINALITY
6 EXPRESSIVENESS

II GOAL DIRECTION – EGO STRENGTH
7 RHYTHM
8 TRI ZONAL DYNAMICS
9 "I" EMPHASIS
10 MIDDLE ZONE HEIGHT
11 FIRMNESS OF DUCTUS

III ORIENTATION TOWARD OTHERS & THE WORLD
12 NATURALNESS SPONTANEITY
13 GARLANDS
14 SLOWNESS TO SPEED
15 HORIZONTAL EXPANSION
16 THREAD
17 RIGHTWARD TREND
18 LEFT MARGIN

IV EMOTIONAL RELEASE
19 CONNECTEDNESS
20 0 TO 5 FLUCTUATION TO 6 TO 10 IRREGULARITY
21 LINEAR - 0 TO 5 PICTORIAL - 6 - 10
22 SHARPNESS - 0 - 5 PASTOSITY - 6 - 10
23 MEAGERNESS - 0 - 5 FULLNESS - 6 - 10

V LIBIDO – ENERGY – DRIVES
24 LOWER ZONE LENGTH
25 LOWER ZONE ELABORATION
26 PRESSURE
27 LEFTWARD TREND

VI REPRESSIONS
28 COVERING STROKES
29 NARROWNESS OF LETTERS
30 RIGIDITY - 10 - 6 FLEXIBILITY - 5 - 0

VII INHIBITIONS – OVER CONTROL
31 RIGHT MARGIN
32 LEFT RIGHT SLANT
33 ARCADES
34 CONTRACTION RELEASE
35 DISTANCE BETWEEN LETTERS 10 = CLOSEST
36 ANGULARITY

VIII CONTROL
37 SLANT CONSISTENCY
38 SPACE BETWEEN WORDS 10 = WIDEST
39 ALIGNMENT CONTROL
40 REGULARITY

Figure 151

Courtesy of Daniel Anthony

Note Anthony's extreme frankness. See how he zeroes in on the writer's outstanding traits.

Every specimen of handwriting is as unique as the writer. To understand the whole person, you must therefore fit the pieces of puzzle together to make a logical whole. This requires a painstaking, error-free analysis, which forces you to interpret the most subtle signs. Lastly, be aware of your responsibility. Never make a statement without graphic proof and never bluff when you are unsure. The ethics of graphology forbid talking over your findings, unless you were hired to do so. (We discuss this in the chapter which follows.)

9

The Application of Graphology

We have seen, at the beginning of this book, how a graphologist can help you determine the most suitable companion or lover among many choices. In fact, after carefully reading (and rereading) this book, you should be able to take a batch of handwriting samples and choose among them one or two ideal persons. (The ideal varies, of course. In the case of the woman doctor in the introduction, some of the most desirable traits were stability, reliability, culture, and a healthy libido.)

You will do better in your analysis—and will be on safer ground—if you gain some experience analyzing many handwriting samples of friends, associates and acquaintances. A man I know, a department store executive, asked a number of his colleagues for samples and carefully looked over handwritten office memos. He did this during a period of a full year because he wanted more graphological experience. One day the executive had an opportunity to study the writing of a superior, a vice president, with whom he could not get along. There was so much conflict between the two men that the younger executive's job was shaky. The handwriting told the amateur graphologist that his boss was an insecure person who craved admiration, flattery and understanding. This sudden insight saved the executive's position at the store.

To be sure, you will gain psychological advantage when you use graphology to understand what goes on within people. We have seen how an analysis of Rita R.'s handwriting brought out deficiencies that would have prevented a happy marriage. (Compatibility studies are also a big part of the field.) A deeper understanding of the 45-year-old woman in Figure 150 would override all superficial impressions—her outer beauty, her amiable, intelligent conversation, and so on. If materialism and a gold-digging tendency turn you off, none of her other traits—her energy or artistic sense—or her strength—would compensate.

Thanks to graphology, young people are helped to understand their parents, and vice versa. The generation gap disappears. Two friends can get to know each other's motivations. Sexual partners can understand their needs better, too. Conversely, a good graphologist (and even this book) may alert you to sexual malfunctions.

Graphology in Business and Industry

I know of businessmen who use graphology before making a loan or before confirming a person's employment. There are many new graphologists who advertise their services to professionals who want to know their staff a little better. If you have enough experience and are sure of your ground, you can contact personnel managers and other top echelon people who hire others and offer your services as a graphologist. You can also write to some of these people. You may at first work on a part-time basis.

European industry has long relied on graphologists. If you have studied enough samples (and have taken enough graphology courses) you too may be able to pick up some corporate clients. This obviously takes: 1) a sound knowledge of graphology; 2) sales ability and poise; 3) knowledge of the companies you are dealing with; 4) knowledge of psychology; and 5) knowledge of the qualities expected for each position to be filled.

The pay for practitioners (including a convincing newcomer) is excellent. Naturally, it takes more than book knowledge. To succeed you need maturity, life experience, sensitivity, and a deep understanding of human beings as well.

After some studies in Germany and Switzerland—and an almost obsessive interest in handwriting—the author helped various British firms select clerks. The companies expected no initiative from these employees, only self-discipline, honesty and industry. My task of selecting people was thus made fairly easy. I wrote a one-page analysis about each individual.

Daniel Anthony starts with an ingenious list of traits, which he obtains from long discussions with a client. For an insurance company in need of salesmen, Anthony came up with this fool-proof list:

- Ambition
- Competitive nature
- Enthusiasm and persuasiveness
- Emotional stability
- Adjustment to job
- Intelligence
- Originality and creativity
- Drive for self realization and ego fulfillment
- Goal direction
- Leadership ability
- Economic success motivation
- Perseverance and resilience
- Physical energies and psychic motivators
- Sociability
- Nagging aspirations
- Willpower and push
- Positive self-defense mechanism

Anthony's total evaluation form is a very thorough analysis of what the life insurance business generally considers to be the most valuable assets of a potential life insurance salesman, largely because it was based upon the actual experiences of many life insurance companies and hundreds of men who succeeded or failed. On the basis of the handwriting, Anthony writes an analysis. He predicts a grade from A to E for a man to be hired, or he advises not to hire. In some cases he predicts failure. Anthony proved to be right 83 percent of the time, over a long period.

There are other graphologists who leave the decision to the employer whether a person should or should not be hired. In the same sense, some companies hire certain people anyway, ignoring the graphologist's advice. Sometimes the personnel managers are honest enough to admit their mistake. One executive had hired a sales engineer despite warnings of dangers ahead, as seen through the applicant's handwriting.

"The impressive qualifications and references produced by this man," the executive's letter later said, "were wrong. And your analysis hit him right on the head. He lasted exactly four weeks before we were forced to ask him to move along. I just thought you would be interested."

Some novice graphologists simplify their work by creating a shorter form than Anthony's, listing various traits (reliability, honesty, intelligence, discipline) and then placing checkmarks behind each characteristic. (One form per handwriting.) Such simplified forms are easily understood by the client and, while they pay much less, can lead to more business.

The use of graphologists is now more widespread than the uninformed may think. If a firm doubts the value of graphology, you can name the following true to life examples:

A leading San Francisco stockbroker employs a handwriting expert to analyze all potential employees.

A large bank in Boston has rejected all other psychological tests in favor of graphology for analyzing its personnel.

The editor of a leading New York City daily newspaper refuses to hire persons without first having their handwriting analyzed.

Keep in mind that you can build up a practice right in your own home. Your only needs are a sound knowledge of graphology, a letterhead, and a typewriter. Whenever you are in doubt about a script, you can always consult books like this one.

Advanced graphologists profit by selling a program to industry, offering analysis of prospective employees. Here is how a woman graphologist tells it: "Companies which test prospective employees extensively," she explained, "use my analyses as a supplement to their regular testing programs. The obvious advantage is that the applicant does not know he is participating. Resentment, nervousness, and other possible unfavorable reactions to testing therefore do not cloud this phase of the procedure."

Anthony once received a long-distance call from the head of a large U.S. corporation. The president just wanted to confirm a hunch derived from an analysis: The man being considered for a key, high-paying post was indeed an alcoholic. None of the company's initial background checks discerned what the eyes of the graphologist picked up.

Vocational Guidance

Many graphologists set up shop in schools where they offer to help chart a young person's professional chances. Like compatibility counselling for men and women, vocational counselling is not at all difficult for the expert.

Felix Klein of New York, for instance, always devotes a portion of his time to guiding young adults, those in college, or those already in their fields. An example of this was a young scientist who came to him, unhappy with his profession. Klein analyzed his handwriting and determined that the man had a talent for writing. Following a suggestion, the young scientist applied for a job with a magazine and is now a leading writer of science-fiction stories and novels.

Klein's judgment of a person is not only razor sharp, but also well expressed. To illustrate: He wrote the following about one handwriting sample (Figure 152):

Figure 152.

'The writer's outstanding quality combination is her high intelligence and her inability to express her feelings adequately.

The basis for the difference in the development of the above mentioned qualities lies in her high sensitivity. Due to that high sensitivity she is reluctant to seek sufficient contact with people although she has a truly friendly nature and concern for others. She may even appear to be introverted—particularly by those who are not her peers. It is much easier for her to show her friendliness to people of her own age group. The lack of emotional release cries out for a substitute. It is necessary for her to express herself in areas that she can successfully pursue.

Providing that she can catch up with her emotional maturity and thereby experience life fully, she could be a writer. Her handwriting also shows an ability to draw—with an emphasis on realism and fine details. If a commercial field should be indicated because of financial reasons, the drawing of greeting cards with a very fine pen seems a strong possibility. I do feel that additional training in education could lead to a teacher's license. Once she has established herself in this field, she could very well specialize as a teacher in her own chosen field.

"Other professional fields indicated are: Analytical research, scientific research and editing.

Such insight is the norm and not the exception, and many readers should be able to write similar short narratives after seeing enough handwriting specimens.

Teaching Graphology

Some people are gifted teachers. They like to share knowledge with others and enjoy the authority of standing before a class. The instruction of graphology is not as lucrative as working with industry, but it has its own special rewards.

Graphology lends itself to teachings and opportunity knocks everywhere throughout North America. Anthony, who teaches at the New School in New York, is an example and now other colleges are in search of instructors, especially in the midwest, the west, and the pacific northwest. Adult education programs, "free universities," adult night schools maintained by cities, and senior citizen programs can all be persuaded to present a graphology course. Only a small portion of these programs now offer classes.

You can also attract students to your own home. I know many who do so. (One of the best known instructors in the eastern United States is Virginia Chafin, who uses her private home in Pennsylvania.)

You can advertise your class in the classified sections of newspapers. Usually such ads draw a dozen or more students. I have also met graphologists who contact apartment houses where they give a free lecture in the recreation room. At the end of the lecture, there are usually enough people signed up for a course to make it profitable. (Public speaking in front of large groups can also be profitable.)

Other graphologists utilize the display ads of regional magazines. Here is a sample from a publication in Denver, Colorado. The ad was enormously effective.

> *WHAT RECESSION?*
>
> Graphologists are now earning $300 each week—and more—at ski resorts, on cruise ships, as personnel consultants to top firms.
>
> Learning handwriting analysis can make you a highly paid professional, while clueing you in to your own hidden potentials and telling you what you really want to know about the people in your life (everything from honesty to I.Q.).
>
> Now G.S., executive director of the Rocky Mountain Graphology Association, is offering classes in this fascinating science. With a background in clinical psychology, Ms. S. is recognized as one of America's leading authorities in Graphology. Her 20-week course gives you over 70 hours of in-depth training.

This same woman, like many of her colleagues, has no trouble getting on many television shows to drum up publicity.

On a more serious level, the New School in New York offers "Graphology II" and "Graphology III" for those who complete the beginner's course. Such university classes are an excellent way to sharpen your own teaching skills.

No doubt the most financially successful operators are the people who give correspondence courses at $650 each. However, no respected graphologist recommends this scheme of the International Graphoanalysis Society. It is too expensive, and its certification only indicates that someone had the money to buy the overpriced course.

The Use of Graphology with Delinquents

During recent years a new brand of graphology developed rapidly, providing extra income for some specialists who work with juveniles. Social welfare agencies, judges and psychiatrists often find work for graphologists.

One of the experts in this field is Mary De Lapp of Boulder, Colorado. She studied young people's handwriting for many years before approaching juvenile authorities. To prove the validity of graphology, Mrs. De Lapp made a comparative study of 100 girls and boys: 25 girls in trouble with the law; 25 average girls; and the same number of boys. She found some interesting differences in their nature and emotional adjustment traits. It gave her a greater understanding of young offenders.

For instance, the troubled children showed a trait of defiance greater than those not in trouble. The delinquents also showed a higher degree of manual dexterity, indicating they might be misguided in school. In fact, many were school dropouts. Their ages ranged from 12 to 28. Mary De Lapp does not see the children. Each week she receives the samples in the mail, analyzes them carefully, and then turns her findings over to Judge Horace Holmes who reviews them, along with results of other tests. The information helps him decide which way the children should go—home, to a detention home, or to a vocational school.

This analyst is moderately well paid for her specialized work, which she finds deeply satisfying. In addition to analysis, Mary De Lapp also sets up courses for other handwriting analysts interested in taking up the speciality. Such courses could work well elsewhere in North America. Mrs.

De Lapp's workshop curriculum includes data on how to interest juvenile courts in her ideas, how to deal with judges, and how to work with schools and certain legal questions.

Handwriting analysis has also found its way into adult prisons as a rehabilitation method. Graphology studies the inner conflicts and special problems of criminals and assists them with self-analysis. Graphologists thus chart attitude changes among convicts.

This scientific method is being used in three major Kentucky prisons: Kentucky State Reformatory in La Grange; Blackburn Correctional Institution in Lexington; and Kentucky Correctional Institute for Women in Pewee Valley.

Graphology in the Courts

Experienced graphologists have long assisted the legal profession. The word of the graphologist in court is treated with the same weight as that of any other expert witness. The graphologist testifies on every type of signature that can be disputed, be it on a will, mortgage, deed, note or wiretap authorization.

Unfortunately, this specialized knowledge is hard to come by and only few schools teach it. One of the few in New York gives you a good clue to this highly advanced topic via the following course description:

> Graphology VII: Handwriting Identification; Forensic Expertise; Advanced Workshop in the Psychology of Handwriting
> Daniel S. Anthony
>
> Open only to students who have satisfactorily completed at least three semesters in Graphology at The New School. Seven sessions cover the investigation and identification of suspect, questioned and/or anonymous handwriting and signatures; methods of procuring appropriate standards; techniques in microscopic examination, comparison and detection; preparation of reports of findings and organizing documents in exhibits for court presentation and testimony as an expert witness. Texts: *Law of Disputed and Forged Documents* by J. Newton Baker; *Suspect Documents* by Wilson R. Harrison; *Scientific Examination of Documents* by Ordway Hilton; *Questioned Documents*, by Albert S. Osborn, and others.

Here is no doubt the most lucrative branch of the profession, and perhaps the hardest to get into. It is also the most controversial, according to legal expert Felix Lehmann of New York City. One recent case in the courts involved a person who disguised his handwriting, then denied that the signature on a contract was his own. Lehmann proved that the signature was indeed legitimate and his client won the case. Recently he was on a case in which he identified checks in an amount well over $100,000 as forgeries.

Lehmann points out that in court cases involving handwriting identification, there are two experts "pitted against each other." His own attitude is that the handwriting analyst "should have the moral certainty that he's defending the truth—whether or not he's under oath." If Lehmann does not have this certainty, he does not take the case. This graphologist regrets that the courts will have nothing to do with character analysis, only with handwriting identification, an attitude Lehmann does not fully agree with because psychological factors like stress, fear, and excitement, can bring on sudden graphic changes. An analyst trained in the psychology of handwriting can use his knowledge to identify two apparently different writings as being from the same hand if the reason for the change is psychological.

The Future of Graphology

To my mind, the future of graphology has already begun with two people you should know about. One is the late Dr. Alfred Kanfer, a European graphologist who worked with the Strang Clinic of Preventive Medicine in New York. He found that magnifying handwriting samples 1000 times gave him a clue to the start of cancer. His was a radical discovery which received further study after his death.

The second innovator was Paul de Ste. Colombe, who, in the footsteps of several French psychiatrists, broadened the theory of "graphotherapy," and explained it with the following:

> Graphotherapy undertakes to break undesirable habits which the hand follows as it writes, replacing them through repetitious exercise with desirable graphic habits. The hand, if you will, is retrained in specific writing gestures.
>
> Handwriting exercises have much in common with the finger exercises employed in learning to play the piano. In the latter case, as long as the pianist must consciously think where to place each finger on the keyboard as he reads the music, he proceeds slowly and painfully, making errors. It is

> only after repetitious practice, when his fingers respond automatically and without conscious attention, that he can perform as an accomplished artist. In graphotherapy, the goal is achieved when the desired handwriting change has passed the state of conscious application and imitation, becoming automatic and normal to the hand.
>
> The time required varies with the individual, because it is easier for some people than for others to break a habit. Another factor is how deeply entrenched the particular habit is, and whether it is a dominant or minor characteristic. Average cases range from two to six months. The change can be facilitated by faithful application, but it never can be hurried. It takes patience, courage, and the determination to continue as long as necessary to accomplish the aim.

Ste. Colombe cited numerous examples of succesful treatment. He produced handwritings of young people, for instance, whose laziness gave way to industry. He worked with a woman who became calm after years of nervousness.

Perhaps most important, graphology has improved its credibility, thanks to practitioners like Daniel Anthony who lectured at Harvard and now teaches extensively.

Predictions: More and more companies will come into the graphological fold; more and more couples will have their writing analyzed before marriage; more men and women will investigate potential partners. More and more good graphologists will be available.

It is a bright future.

Bibliography

Casewit, Curtis. *Freelance Writing: Advice From the Pros.* New York, New York: Macmillian.

Colombe, Paul de Ste. *Grapho-Therapeutics.* Hollywood, California: Laurida Books.

Pulver, Dr. Max. *Symbolik Der Handschrift.* Munich, West Germany: Kindler Publishing.

Teltscher, Dr. H.O. *Handwriting—Revelation of the Self.* New York, New York: Hawthorn Books.

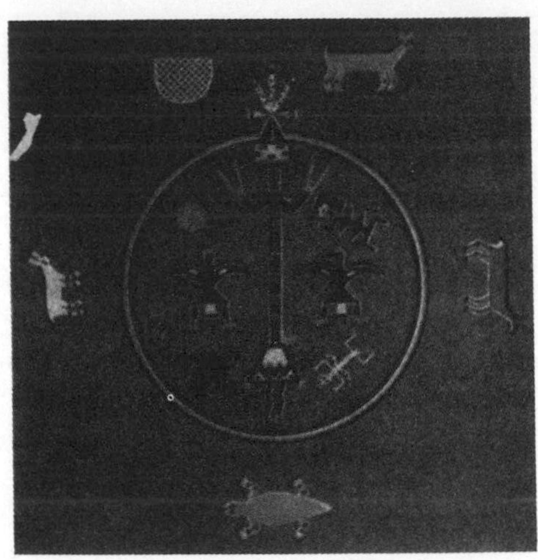

INDIAN MEDICINE POWER

Brad Steiger

According to Brad Steiger, medicine power, a way of life elemental to Native American heritage and contemporary religious practice, may well be the unique mystical experience and the proper spiritual path for our continent. At the core of medicine power is the quest for wisdom of mind and body. Men and women pursuing this quest are often great healers, but the true meaning of the term "medicine" extends beyond the arts of healing to include clairvoyance, precognition and unity with nature and the great spirit.

Indian Medicine Power includes extensive interviews with contemporary medicine men and women from numerous tribes. Steiger himself was initiated into the medicine lodge of the Wolf Clan of the Seneca tribe, given the name of Hat-yas-swas (He Who Testifies) and charged with the search and sharing of universal truths.

The truths of medicine power shared in this book include the nature and importance of the vision quest, the belief in total partnership with the World of Spirits, awareness of one's place in the web of life and the power of walking in balance with the earth.

As Donna Linstead, a member of the Cree Tribe and professor of Native American Studies, says in her introduction: "*Indian Medicine Power* provides each reader with a path from yesterday to tomorrow that allows for individual growth, awareness, and an accessibility to the ancient mysteries that continue to be practiced today. Brad Steiger has demonstrated an uncommon insight into the sacred belief systems of the Amerindian."

ISBN 0-914918-65-6
240 pages, paper

$12.95